AN ENTREPRENEUR'S FAST-START GUIDE TO

MARKET RESEARCH ON A SHOESTRING

Get a Reality Check on
Your Big Idea for Less than $100

NAEEM ZAFAR

University of California, Berkeley—Haas Business School
www.Startup-Advisor.com

Market Research on a Shoestring:
Get a Reality Check on Your Big Idea for Less than $100

Published by:

Five Mountain Press

Five Mountain Press
Cupertino California USA
info@FiveMountainPress.com
www.FiveMountainPress.com

ISBN 13: 978-0-9823420-4-6
ISBN 10: 0-9823420-4-7

Printed in the United States of America

Other Books from the Author (Available at www.FiveMountainPress.com**)**

- The Entrepreneur's Legal Guide to Starting Up: 35 Little-Known Facts, Secrets, Techniques, and Tricks to Making Sure You Get Every Penny's Worth of Value from Your Lawyer

- Finance Essentials for Entrepreneurs: A Simple Guide to Creating and Understanding Financial Statemenets for Your Business

This book is for those starting a new venture or thinking about starting a new business. It builds on the concepts discussed in my book *The 7 Steps to a Successful Startup*, providing practical "how-to" advice for the first three steps of the seven-step process.

For more, see www.Startup-Advisor.com.

Table of Contents

The Purpose of This Book

Most people would never think of heading out for a long hike in the wilderness without some preparation. They would check out a map, inquire about where the trail leads, or find out whether it will bring them back to the starting location. They would probably carry water and some food with them. They may even talk to other hikers who have walked the same trail.

But for some reason, most entrepreneurs don't bother with similar preparation, even though a lot more than a day outdoors is at stake. They get excited about their ideas, jumping right into their execution and implementation. Some people rush to incorporate their businesses and spend thousands of dollars on legal fees. Some people jump to patent their ideas (and also end up spending thousands). Many even quit their jobs to pursue their dreams. They often find themselves without either a market or customers, despite several months of hard work. They pay a high price for this journey in terms of their time, their savings, and the toll taken on their personal relationships.

Four Simple Diagrams!

It doesn't have to be this way. Smart entrepreneurs take a different path. They discover the customers first. They arrive at the starting point with a clear understanding of what they should be developing and delivering to their customers—who will then be eager to hand over their money. If you follow the techniques and advice in this book, you too will significantly improve your chances of success. Just four diagrams will give you the data you need. Once you can draw these four diagrams, you have completed your market research and are ready to begin building your business!

In this book, I will walk you step-by-step through the techniques and methods of conducting this essential research for practically free.

Research Your Business Model before You Start!

This may be shocking, but I can guarantee that you can have a business that can reach $10 million in revenue within six months. Surprised? Think about this: What if you sold dollar bills for 98 cents? Your business would be sure to take off. Your revenue would rise rapidly, but it would be a lousy business—you would lose money on every transaction. This is exactly what happens to a business with a poorly formulated business model. Many entrepreneurs don't understand this concept until they have spent months developing a product and trying to start a company.

If you are trying to decide whether it is really worth your time and energy to start a new venture or business, read this book. You might think that many people can use your product or service. But you need to find out with as much certainty as possible whether there is really a group of people **who really need your product**. Starting a company without sufficient market research can lead to unnecessary hardship, not to mention great risk to your personal wealth and health. You are about to start a long journey. You want to make sure that this journey leads to a clear and happy destination. True, you may take many detours. You may even change your destination at some point. But having clarity about your destination can save you time and money—and make the journey more enjoyable.

Performing market research and gaining such clarity is not difficult. For most businesses, spending two to four months doing market research and discerning "deep customer needs" will allow you to learn just about anything you need to know **before** you quit your day job and launch headlong into your startup.

I have been involved in six startups myself and have counseled hundreds of entrepreneurs who were somewhere in the process of starting a company. (See my bio at the end of this book to learn more about my experience.) I have seen more than one startup derail in the absence of sufficient market research. The result of insufficient market research: the entrepreneur-owner lacked clarity about his or her target audience. In many cases, that entrepreneur was going after too small a market.

I know that you will find this book useful. I hope that you read it carefully and share with me your own experiences and tips. I want to share them with others who seek to start a fulfilling and enjoyable journey: a life of entrepreneurship!

Section 1

Demystifying Market
Research

This section will discuss why market discovery is so important for starting a new business. Whether you are starting a high-technology venture or a restaurant, the principals of market research apply equally. Whatever business you are in, you need to discover as much about your customers as you can, including their habits and buying patterns.

This knowledge will give you the "unfair advantage" that allows you to make the decisions you need to succeed in business. Once you have studied the landscape and carved out a position for yourself, you will have a much better chance of attracting both customers and investors. Achieving clarity about **how** you will make money will make you much more likely actually to make money. In this section, I will outline exactly what we mean by the term "market research." In subsequent sections, I will outline how to conduct market research in the most cost-efficient manner possible.

"But," you may ask, "how will I know that I have achieved this clarity and am ready to move forward?"

The answer is straightforward. I have synthesized my years of experience into four simple diagrams. If you can draw them with clarity and can substantiate the data behind them, then you are ready to forge ahead!

Chapter 1

What is Market Research?

MARKET RESEARCH IS an essential process for every start-up—but many entrepreneurs do it too late. They wait until after quitting their job and starting a company, when they are already spending money rapidly. Smart entrepreneurs, on the other hand, do the bulk of their market research while they are still shaping their ideas, when they most likely still have other sources of income. I suggest that you do the latter! The specific steps I explain below will make doing so easier.

You need to spend some time discovering your market before you embark on this long journey. Why? Two reasons—one, to maximize the odds of your success; and two, to minimize the toll the process can take on your finances and relationships.

Market discovery consists of five main elements, also known as **Five Questions All Entrepreneurs Must Answer Before Starting a Business:**

1) Do you fulfill an unmet need, or do you have a solution looking for a problem?
2) Who most acutely experiences this unmet need?
   (This question addresses market segmentation.)
3) How many people occupy this particular market?
   (This question addresses market size.)
4) Who else is trying to fill this need, and how will you be different from them in your customer's eyes?
   (This question addresses your competitive positioning in the marketplace.)
5) How will you make money?
   (This question addresses your business model.)

Your research will net you the ability to draw the four diagrams shown below. If you can accurately draw these four pictures, you will have found the kind of knowledge that separates "fundable" entrepreneurs from others. You will be equipped with a *profound understanding of the dynamics of your market*! This knowledge will command the respect of your investors.

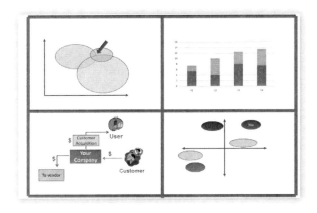

These four pictures represent all the market research that you need to do. Once you can draw them accurately, you have finished your market research! Then you can move on to the next project.

Let me explain what each of these four pictures means.

1.1 Segmentation: Which Market Segment Will I Start with First?

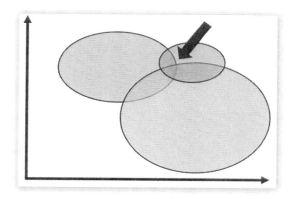

You must find out about the people who can benefit from your product or service. Who are they? Which segment of that group needs you more than the others? The red arrow above points to the group that most needs your product or service. You will start selling to them first because they have indicated to you that their need is urgent, immediate, and significant. They are willing to spend money **right now** to solve their problem.

This is the essence of market segmentation. You have a very limited budget. You CANNOT go after everyone who may eventually need you. **You must own a "beachhead"**—an area in which you become the king of the hill, whatever that hill may be! Once you own that segment, you can attack adjacent segments and keep growing your business. But knowing which segment to go after first is an essential market research question that you will have to answer.

1.2 Market Size: How Big Is the Total Market, and What Piece of That Market Can I Serve?

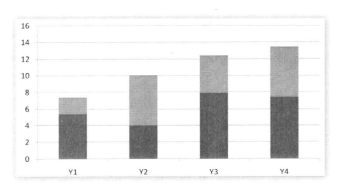

This picture will help you understand how big an opportunity you are chasing. You need to know how big the market is and how big a slice of that market you need to succeed. Each tricolored bar indicates the total available market. Of these three colors, you are concerned with the color that represents your serviceable market segment. This chart helps you understand and convey to your investors the size of your achievable target market.

For example, let's say you have a language product geared toward new immigrants to the U.S. Each bar indicates all the languages spoken by immigrants in a given year. The blue bar represents Chinese-speaking immigrants (who happen to be your initial target). This chart quickly tells the reader that your total target population is growing. Someday, you may be able to market to every major language, but for now, you are focused on one—and thanks to this chart, you can clearly see the amount of growth in that market.

1.3 Business Model: How Will I Make Money?

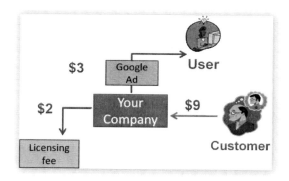

This picture displays your business model. It answers the following questions:
- How will you make money?
- How much money will you make per transaction?

This diagram shows you more about the "characters" in the "play" you are directing and how they interact with each other. Such clarity will not come easily, but once you are able to draw this diagram for your business, you will know that you are ready to proceed.

(**Remember**: your customer may or may not be the product's user. I will explain this concept in more detail later.)

1.4 Market Positioning: How Will I Make Myself Stand Out to My Customers?

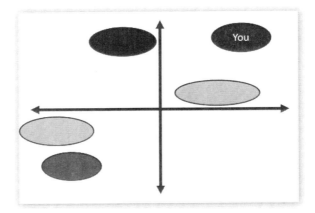

This picture helps you understand who else is trying to serve the same need as you and how you will appear different to your users and customers. You choose the labels on both the x-axis and the y-axis—they will be different for each company. They may be "Manual" versus "Automated," or "Expensive" versus "Inexpensive," or "Super-friendly" versus "Not Friendly." The labels will be specific to your business and the various ways in which you want to differ from other players. Make sure the labels represent the ways in which you want to differentiate yourself from others. This picture helps your audience understand how your company is unique.

Chapter 2

Why Do I Need to Do Market Research?

YOU ARE ABOUT to commit several months—if not years—of your life and a significant portion of your personal savings to pursue your dream. Therefore, you must be as certain as possible that enough people really want and need to use your product. Consumers must have enthusiasm for your product or service and must be willing to pay for it, even **before** you design, manufacture, and market it.

As you engage in this process, you may discover a large group of people that can use your product. Great—but you must dig deeper. You need to discern, from all the people who can possibly use this

Don't I Need the Product First?

When Greg Gioanforte was starting Right Now Technologies in 1999, he locked himself in his bedroom for three months and made 400 calls to potential customers. He explained his plans to offer CRM (Customer Relationship Management) software on a web-based model, what is now called SaaS (Software as a Service). He said the product would be available in six months and asked if they would like to sign up.

product, which sliver of customers needs it the most. Who are they? How can you reach them? Are there enough of them to enable you to turn a profit? (More about that last part in a later chapter.)

A smart entrepreneur must be able to answer these questions before he or she progresses too far in the development of a product or service. Of the hundreds of entrepreneurs I have met and mentored, I have coached only a few—perhaps less than 10%—who really understood the need to find buyers before getting started. Those who were not aware of this need struggled to succeed with their product.

Doing your homework early offers huge benefits. Most entrepreneurs get very excited about their ideas; talk to a few friends to make sure they are also excited; and then spend several months creating, making, and polishing their products. By the time each person begins to sell the product, however, it has missed the mark—it's too late, too big, too expensive, or missing certain essential features. There are dozens of reasons why your product or service

---

Don't I Need the Product First?-continued

He heard an earful—everything from "This is a stupid idea!" to "I have been waiting for a product like this!" Customers asked for certain features. They told him how they would shape the product if they had the chance.

After three months, Greg had signed up 40 customers. He then locked himself in his room again for three months. He had the first version of his software product ready for installation in at the end of that time, just as he had promised his customers. Guess how the company did?

Right Now Technologies is now a publicly traded company, and Greg is still the CEO. He did exactly what I am talking about: he gauged the market first, and then he developed his product. This is how smart entrepreneurs start a company!

might not succeed. Market research can help you avoid unnecessary failures.

You must be sure to address these questions: Who needs you? How badly do they need you?

Having clarity early, even if it your vision changes later, helps you make smarter, better decisions. Once you know that you have a sizeable market, you can create a product to meet that market's needs.

2.1 What question are we really trying to answer?

Before you can formulate your questions, you must be clear about the the purpose of your research. Its purpose is to understand the customer's unmet need. Thus, a successful entrepreneur asks the following questions in a way that fits the context of his or her business:

1) Who are the customers? Who will pay me money?
2) How many such people exist out there?
3) Who will use this product (or service)? What are they looking for? How badly do they need it?
4) Why will they buy from me?
5) What is the buying process, and who needs to approve this purchase?
6) What are their selection criteria?
7) At what price point will they decide to buy?
8) Why would they not buy?

9) Why have they not bought this solution from someone else until now?

10) Who will be my initial target, given my marketing budget?

Can someone achieve such clarity without starting a business, getting a business license, or incorporating? Yes—this is EXACTLY what smart entrepreneurs do! Such research will tremendously increase the odds that your endeavor will be successful.

More details on this process and the 28 crucial questions you must ask yourself are provided in section 5.5.

We all have different tastes. We all have different ideas about what is necessary and important to our lives. Often, entrepreneurs believe that they have a great idea for a product, only to later discover that no one else thinks so. Researching the market ahead of time will save you unnecessary pain and hassle.

How Much Market Research Is Necessary?

I am not asking you to do years of complex research and book reading. I am simply asking you to talk to a few of your customers before you try to solve a problem that you suspect they may have!

The business world's ever-increasing complexity and competitiveness makes market research more necessary today than ever before. Why? Doing your homework ahead of time increases your decision-making confidence. It also reduces your risks, ensuring that your customers will be satisfied once product development is completed. It can also be used to test new concepts, check pricing plans, and track trends in the markets.

Chapter 3

The Elements of Market Research

THIS CHAPTER DEALS with the different tactics an entrepreneur can apply when conducting market research. This is the process of discovering your market—and, most importantly, discovering your customers. What do they really want? What words do they use to express their wants? Where will you find them? How will you talk to them?

In this chapter, I will discuss four ways to collect this data. The next chapter covers in greater detail how to complete each step.

3.1 Key elements

1) Conduct customer interviews
2) Conduct online surveys
3) Use Google AdWords to conduct research
4) Use Twitter to conduct market research
5) Use publicly available data on the Internet

I suggest that you start with some one-on-one interviews. As you expand your research, you will find that certain methods work best for your particular product or service. The diagram below is a good way to look at the process:

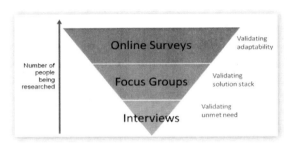

As you progress in your research, you will establish and validate the unmet need that you are striving to meet and then start thinking about possible solutions to that unmet need. Then, to validate your thinking, you will need to speak with or survey a larger group of potential customers.

In my experience, the best entrepreneurs do not hire any staff members, write a single line of code, or develop anything before having "sold" their products. I am not talking about cheating the customer; in fact, I am talking about seeking your customer's input by firing their imaginations. Successful entrepreneurs convince their customers to buy into the solution to their as-of-yet-unmet problem, gleaning information about how they will buy it and at what price. You can tell customers that the product is under development and will be available within a certain time frame. If people truly have an unmet need, they will be willing to tell you what it is. You must establish that this unmet need actually exists. **You cannot delegate this part of the research**!

3.2 Talk to Your Customers and Users

The most important part of primary market research is actually talking to a few of your users and customers. This may seem like a difficult step. You may feel uncomfortable finding these people. You might feel like a cheap salesperson trying to sell door-to-door. But nothing could be further from the truth. You are a helper. You are trying to solve (or uncover) a problem. You have nothing to sell yet, so you are just making conversation.

But how does one go about talking to customers? Where do you find these people?

As a rule, I will not allow any of my clients to start a company until they have spoken to at least 10 users and customers. The information gained from these conversations is too important. You must understand what both groups are looking for and why have they not found it.

I suggest you make lists of at least 10 people each from both your professional and

Customers vs. Users

Remember, your customers may not be your product's users. Users use—customers pay. Often they are the same people, but sometimes they are not. Selling technology solutions to hospitals is a good example. Nurses and doctors use the products, but the IT manager is the customer. If you are selling children's products, then parents are the customers. Parents have their own issues and criteria for buying, while children, the users, have their own criteria. You must get to know both constituencies, because you will need to satisfy both of them.

personal worlds. Bring these people together over a casual meal and have an informal discussion about your product idea. Either one-on-one meetings or a group setting will work. I prefer one-on-one meetings; they are more focused and formal, and you will get better data (group dynamics sometimes cause bias to creep in).

If your team includes two or three founders and each of you talks to 10 people in your professional and personal networks, you will already have input from between 40 and 60 additional people. This diversity of opinion, and the richness of data it contains, will factor positively into your business equation.

If your plan is for a business-to-business (B2B) idea, you will need to contact a mix of people consisting of both users and buyers. You can meet these individuals at tradeshows or by calling up businesses that may be interested in your product or service. Most people will give you 20 minutes of their time if you tell them you are doing some market research for a company and want to discuss a few ideas about a product relevant to them.

Your research audience lists will give you a good idea of your target customers. I expect that the number of names on your first list (your professional contacts) will be the longest. The next chapter explains what to say to these people when you meet them.

Chapter 4

How Much to Disclose While Doing Market Research

MISCONCEPTIONS ABOUND on this topic. Many entrepreneurs I talk to are afraid to reveal what they are working on. They fear that their best idea will be "stolen," and they talk about filing patents before talking to anyone. Let me shed some light on this topic.

4.1 How Open Should I Be?

New entrepreneurs often have questions about disclosure, such as, "If I talk to people, how will I keep my idea secret," "should I have them sign a Non-Disclosure Agreement (also known as an NDA)," and "what should I and what shouldn't I talk about?"

Because so much is at stake, you should talk to as many potential customers as possible—between 30 and 100 people, depending on the product or service you are thinking about offering. This research will give you a good sense of what your product or service should or shouldn't be. In addition, I suggest that you consider

Every Idea Can Be Made Better

Remember, all ideas must be chiseled away at—streamlined—to become fundable. Your conversations with users and customers will help shape those ideas. No company I know of has ever gone to production with an idea unchanged from its conception.

Your Idea Should Not Be So Secret

The benefits to talking to as many people as possible about the problem you are solving far outweigh the risk that someone will take your idea. What you do is not the same as how you do it. Focus on talking about the "how" of your idea with relevant people. Look for reactions and feedback, and allow these responses to shape your thinking.

having a customer advisory council. This council should consist of between 5 and 20 customers who are engaged in conversation over the long term. As you make progress, you will need to check back with them from time to time.

Should I keep my idea a secret?

If your idea is so simple that everybody will steal it as soon as you mention it, maybe it's not such a good idea. Ideas are a dime a dozen. The difficult part of any idea is the execution. The real challenge lies in understanding how to design your product or service correctly and then how to create it, sell it, and support it. The advantages offered by receiving meaningful feedback far outweigh the risk that your idea will be stolen.

Most entrepreneurs falter at this point. It's easy to sit down on your couch and come up with dozens of innovative, attractive ideas. The execution is the hard part. Don't be afraid to talk about your idea with relevant people.

4.2 What Should I or Should I Not Talk About?

Obviously, you shouldn't talk to competitors about your idea directly. You also should not talk to people who are not potential users and have no sense of your market's needs. But you should certainly approach people you identify as potential customers or users.

Talk about the "what" and "why" of your product or service. The "how" is something you should hold back until there is a reason to disclose it—and you may never have a valid reason for disclosing it. If the customer wants to talk about how your product works, it is time to introduce a confidentiality agreement or a Non-Disclosure Agreement (NDA) into the conversation. But even if you have someone sign an NDA (templates are available on the Internet), you must ask yourself, "Do I really have the money to sue this person if he or she violates the agreement?"

So, use an NDA as a matter of procedure when talking about product details—but do not be so uneasy that you won't talk to anybody who doesn't sign one. Some people, such as investors, will refuse to sign NDAs. Many larger companies, by policy, will not let their employees sign an NDA (or they might require a person higher in the organization to sign it), because it can

Non-Disclosure Agreements

Non-Disclosure Agreements (NDAs) may seem like a good idea in theory, but they are unrealistic in practice. Venture Capitalists (VCs), as a practice, refuse to sign such agreements. They have plenty of fluidity to choose among deals, and they would rather not feel hassled by some entrepreneur who fears that his idea may be stolen.

Non-Disclosure Agreements (continued)

The bottom line is this: You should ask for a signed NDA if you are going to discuss the "how" part of your idea with the appropriate parties, but you should not ask for one when you discuss the "what" and "why" of your idea. Ultimately, a handshake is what matters. When it comes to confidential information, however, it's necessary to have people sign an NDA and to label your documents as "Confidential."

You can find much more information about these and other legal topics in another book by this author, located at www.Startup-Advisor.com/Lawyer-Guide.html.

create legal liability for the company. If the company is accused of stealing someone's secret, information may be disclosed inappropriately. Keep those conversations informal, fun, and short, and you will have no need to use a non-disclosure or confidentiality agreement.

Patents

If your idea is patentable, don't discuss it in public forums. (Art and knowledge that is publically available cannot be patented.) Discussing your idea with a potential vendor or customer may not be considered public disclosure. Writing about it or presenting it at a conference, on the other hand, can legitimately be considered public disclosure.

I suggest that you apply for a provisional patent application. This inexpensive document preserves your product or service's "invention date" for up to one year, giving you time to prepare and file a proper patent application. You can learn more about provisional patent applications in my above-mentioned book on lawyers.

Market Research Methods

This section outlines five methods you can use to collect information about your customers and markets. Once you have collected the information, you will be able to find meaning in the data.

The five boxes below indicate the steps of the market research process, while the red words underneath outline the techniques for obtaining the answers you need. I also list the specific methods outlined in this section, which you can use to get the information you need. I will explain all of these methods with specific examples in the next few pages.

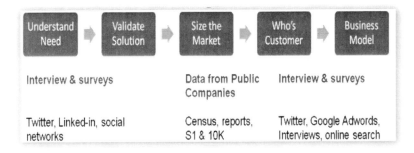

Chapter 5

Conducting Customer Interviews

THE BIGGEST HESITATION I see in entrepreneurs doing market research involves performing interviews. Often they are deathly afraid of starting a conversation with a potential user or customer. But this step is essential, and it must be completed by the company's founders. Don't delegate this job!

"But," you may ask, "where do I find these people?" "I don't know anybody." We will discuss this topic in sections 5.4, 5.7, and 9.5. In addition, all of Chapter 8 is dedicated to finding people with whom you can initiate these conversations. Do not underestimate the power of alumni networks, local groups, nonprofits, and networking events such as trade shows. You will need to pinpoint your outreach targets and keep methodical notes for each interaction about the people you've spoken to as well as what you've learned from the conversations. A methodical, organized entrepreneur has a far better chance at success.

5.1 Start with the End in Sight

You can ignite a customer's imagination by creating a one- or two-page product brochure. Or you can do a mockup of a website, or even a series of hand-drawn sketches, that tells a reader what your service or product would look like if it existed. You may also want to create compelling presentations that help the customer imagine him- or herself using the service or product. These techniques help the customer give you meaningful feedback. Documents or mockups give the customer basic information about the product: what it does, the market holes it fills, and the features it possesses. The entrepreneur is essentially starting by displaying the finished product. Though this approach may seem counterintuitive, it is a very effective technique that can flesh out your thoughts. It helps you be sure that the product idea makes sense to the customers who are ultimately going to pay for it.

Talk to Your Customers!

Customers are your targets. Making a product without garnering their approval or seeking out their perspectives is detrimental to your business. Performing market research and talking to your customers minimizes risk, taking the guesswork out of customer service.

In the next section, however, I will outline one way you must never start your conversation: by talking about YOUR idea. I will explain why this approach is exactly the wrong tack to take!

5.2 Why Talking to Customers is Important

The next step is to start talking to potential customers. It is important to see the world from their perspective. Many of the people who will actually be using your product or service will make their decision without your being physically present to convince them. Some might even make their decision based on what they hear from other people about your product. It's crucial to get inside potential customer's heads; this will allow you to understand what will convince them to buy, even if they never speak to you directly.

Of course, you will not implement everything a potential customer suggests. Your goal is to obtain a 360-degree view of how people will feel about your product or service. So, an important aspect of any new business venture is identifying who will be your customers, how to find them, and what to ask when you meet them.

Most likely, you will not react based on any particular piece of feedback you receive. You will, however, need to be rigorous about discussing and documenting everything you hear in the course of your research. Resist the urge to be defensive about your product or service. You are simply collecting valuable information about what your potential clients need from you and how badly they need your proposed product or service. Then it will be up to you to decide what you can successfully implement.

> **Talk to Your Customers!** (continued)
>
> When it comes to market research, cost is the biggest issue facing most entrepreneurs. Research studies aren't cheap: costs can range from $5,000 to over $100,000. As a bootstrap entrepreneur, you don't have that kind of money. That means you will need to do most of this research at minimal cost, by talking to your customers. Most people should be able to accomplish 70% of what they need by spending less than $1,000. But developing a product and then realizing that you made erroneous assumptions about consumer demand will have a far greater negative financial impact than even the heftiest initial outlay for research studies.

Once you have evaluated the information you receive, the next step is to go back and validate your ideas with 10 or 20 of your most promising potential customers.

The Importance of Market Research in a Recession

These days, consumers are cutting costs left and right. People are not willing to spend money continually on products or services they don't need for everyday living. Uncertainty in the business world has increased. Many companies wrongly believe that market research is not important and should therefore be cut in order to conserve cash.

Slashing market research efforts affects these companies negatively, but many companies don't realize this. According to AdMedia Partners, only 27% of companies are planning to increase their spending on market research in our recession-challenged times.

A Two-Stage Process

There are two stages to the market research process. The first stage involves identifying the product in your own mind and then talking to potential users and customers to better understand the perceived need for this product. These interviews are about discovering unmet consumer needs. You may never even bring up your own ideas about the product or service to customers in this stage.

The second stage involves writing a product brochure or creating a presentation and talking to between 20 and 100 people who may be interested in buying your product or service. During these interviews, you will want to go through a standard set of questions with each person. About 20% of the meetings should be face-to-face; the rest of the discussions can take place over the Internet or by phone. Then, based on the data you collect, you can refine your product idea and perhaps even develop a prototype. Afterwards, you will go back to a subset of the customers you talked to before and obtain their feedback a second time. You should complete all of these steps before you engage in any product development.

5.3 How to Talk to Customers

Many entrepreneurs cringe at the thought of talking to their consumer base. Why? First of all, most entrepreneurs tend to be technically oriented people and are often introverts. And for some entrepreneurs, talking to customers makes them feel sleazy. Many entrepreneurs have no idea what to say to the people who will ultimately be purchasing their products or services.

> **The Importance of Market Research in a Recession (continued)**
>
> **But market research is a long-term investment.** Knowing what your customers want and then shaping your product or service based on their suggestions is even more important in a recession. The time and money you spend on market research will reap rewards down the line!

But sales should not be viewed as sleazy. I believe making sales is one of the noblest and most thrilling parts of entrepreneurship. After all, the focus in sales is on understanding your customers' needs and finding specific ways to help them by filling those needs. You need to sit down and talk to the customers who are interested, or may be interested, in your product.

This is what you are trying to establish:

1) Is there a real unmet need in your product's area, i.e., does you product address an existing problem?
2) How does the customer want to see this problem solved?

3) Why has this problem not been solved until now? What issues are preventing it from being solved?

4) If a solution existed to this problem, what would it look like?

5) Who will use this product (or service)? What are these users looking for? How badly do they want it?

6) What is the buying process for this product? In other words, who will need to approve this purchase?

7) What are the selection criteria for choosing such a product?

8) What price point will make this purchasing decision a no-brainer? At what price point are you likely to find resistance?

9) For what reasons would somebody decide not to buy this product?

10) Why hasn't the customer bought this solution from someone else until now?

11) Who else might be interested in solving this problem?

12) Who in the organization is the most likely to champion solving this problem? Can you get an introduction to them?

A much longer list of questions, along with techniques for asking them, appears in the next section.

You may have noticed that none of these questions forces you to reveal your idea. First you must understand the market's need and establish the process of "selling." Revealing your product first will bias the audience. No one will tell you to your face that they hate your idea; instead, you will receive polite answers that confirm your initial assumptions. Such polite dishonesty begets disaster.

Listen, and learn how your customer thinks. Later on (sometimes later in the same meeting), you may come to stage two of this research and say, "OK, what if such a product did exist? Let me show you a demo [or a sketch/drawing/mockup—or the real thing!], and let's see if this might fit the solution." Just don't start with this offer. Start by asking some version of the 12 questions I outlined above.

Once you've settled down to ask these questions, take out your notepad and pen and begin writing down your customer's thoughts. Ask, "If I developed a product or service that answered your needs, would you be interested in making a purchase?" Listen carefully to the answers! The customer will tell you exactly what you want to know, if you will simply be quiet and listen. You will be tempted several times to chime in and say, "That is exactly what I have developed." Resist the urge—it will derail the conversation, and you will miss out on the chance to ask the remaining questions. To succeed, you must know the answers to those questions.

Such an interview will also net you valuable ideas about how to improve your product or service so that it can better meet the needs of your

Customers Can Tell You More Than You Think!

Smart entrepreneurs and managers can successfully beat their competition by surveying customers and shaping their company based on what the consumers tell them. Explain to your customers how your product or service will benefit them and why they will like it. If your potential customers don't believe you, then you know that your initial plans need to be reshaped. Instead of trying to figure out what your customers think, ask them directly. Direct communication saves you future time and effort and gives your company the competitive advantage it deserves!

customers. Now is not the time to push for a sale. Now is the time to let the customer do the talking.

5.4 Where Do I Find These Customers?

The answer to this question depends on what product or service you are trying to sell; for example, if you are planning to offer a product to web developers, you probably know there are certain places where they hang out. Look for your customers there.

A very good place to find customers is **industry trade shows**. Such shows gather a large group of people who specialize in a field related to your product or service. People go to these events in order to visit with colleagues as well as to check out the competition. Trade shows provide an informal setting for many of the conversations you are seeking. You needn't spend money exhibiting your potential product or service. You can just attend as a visitor and strike up conversations with people as they walk the hallways or take breaks.

You can also find potential customers by simply sitting down and making a list of the companies that may be interested in buying your product. You will actually need to make two lists. The first should consist of your product's users—the people in your target companies who will actually apply your product. For example, if you are selling a software package, the user might be the vice president of engineering, the product marketing folks, the IT manager, or the design engineers. Understanding these individuals' needs is crucial.

You will also need a second list, consisting of your product's purchasers—the people who will actually buy your product for its users. Often the user and the purchaser will be one and the same, but in the corporate world, they are frequently different people. A typical example is hospital-related products. The users are most often nurses and doctors, but the buyer can be a technology manager, chief information officer (CIO), IT manager, or administrator, depending on the product you are selling.

Next, write down where your product's users and buyers are most likely to be found. Trade shows offer particularly good opportunities, because of their informal settings; you will often catch people who are bored and seeking to make conversation. Such moments offer a great time to ask a set of interview questions if you are well prepared and have thought through your questions ahead of time.

If the product is consumer oriented, your task will be easier. You can find people in your circle of friends or family, in public places, in your church or other place of worship, or through groups you belong to. Be tenacious; ask the people you know to be on the lookout for people with whom you can have such conversations. If you don't ask, you shall not receive.

5.5 What to Ask While Doing Research

Deciding what to ask your potential customers is one of the most important aspects of selling a product or service. It is also the point at which many entrepreneurs make mistakes. You must know what to ask in order to successfully discover your market opportunities. Again, I encourage you to perform two phases of market research.

In the first phase, you are simply trying to learn what the unmet need is, without revealing your idea for answering that need. This research will help you understand the unmet need in its raw form. In the second phase, you will be talking to potential customers about how you plan to address their needs, and you will be receiving feedback on the product. This stage will yield specific feedback about implementing the product or service that will ultimately meet the need. How you do this will vary slightly, depending on the product or service you plan to offer.

28 questions to ask when you interview a potential customer

Let's consider some specific examples of questions to ask customers. If you are talking to people about an unmet need, you will want to ask the following:

1) **What keeps you awake at night?**
   (This question comes after you have framed the area of the unmet need.)

2) **What are the two or three things you worry most about?**

(This seems similar to question number one, but it may reveal some new information, perhaps an adjacent area that you may be contemplating entering.)

If your product has something to do with internet security for companies, for example, you will target chief information officers (CIOs), webmasters, or IT managers. You will need to frame your discussion by saying, "I am conducting some research for an internet security product. I would like to get your reaction concerning the two, three, or four things that keep you awake at night." These nagging concerns will be the areas your customer is willing to spend money on to address.

Simply write down their answers. Maybe your target area appears as one of the top five concerns, or maybe it isn't mentioned. *Now is not the time to try and educate your interviewees regarding your big idea.* This time is intended to help you to get a better idea about the issues on *their* minds!

Once you have pinpointed some of your customers' concerns, you can ask another set of questions, including:

3) **How have you tried to solve this problem?**

4) **What companies or products have you looked at to solve this problem?**

5) **Why haven't you bought those products or services to fill that need?**

6) **What were your concerns about those products or services?**
(Maybe it was the product's price, maturity, or availability— or maybe the right product simply wasn't on the market.)

7) **Where do you normally look when seeking products like these?**
(The answer will help you understand where you will be promoting your product down the road.)

8) **What is a fair price range for such products?**

9) **What is your budget?**

10) **Has your budget been approved within your company?**

11) **Are you looking to spend the money this year, this quarter, this month?**

12) **If you were not to be able to spend money to buy a new solution, what other alternatives have you looked at?**

13) **If you did explore these alternatives, why haven't they worked out?**

14) **Who will make this decision to purchase a new product?**

15) **What is the purchasing process (in your company or household)?**

16) **Who has to approve a purchase of this amount?**

These questions conclude the first set of queries in Phase One of your business discussion. Depending on how responsive your interviewee is, you may or may not go on to the Phase Two questions. Regardless, Phase One is necessary for understanding the customer without giving away any of your own ideas. It offers you a chance to obtain an unadulterated view of customers' thoughts and how they perceive the situation.

In Phase Two of the conversation, you might impose a hypothetical:

17) **What if a product or service like this existed?**
(Now you are talking about your own product idea.)

18) **How would you feel if it had some of the following features?**
(You would then list the features of your product or service.)

19) **Would you consider implementing it?**
(This question may be too aggressive, however, and the customer's guard may go up. You may want to do more market research before asking this question or simply withdraw the query and move on.)

20) **These are some of the aspects or features of this product. What other features would you like to see?**

21) **What features must it have before you would even consider making a purchase?**

22) **What features would be nice, making it more attractive for you?**

23) **What is a suitable price for this product or service?** (The answers you get back may not be directly applicable to your product, but depending on your customer's responsiveness to the conversation, you may want to throw this question in.)

24) **What price would you consider too high, and why?**

25) **What price would you consider a bargain, and why?**

You should be recording or taking extensive notes on the conversation. I suggest you make a recording so that you can go back and listen to the interviewee's responses again. You may also want to ask some additional questions:

26) **Where would people buy this product?**

27) **How is such a product typically purchased?**

28) **When was the last time you looked for such a product?**

These sample questions offer excellent ways to start a good conversation with each interviewee. Once you have had five or six conversations, you'll be able to refine your questioning.

Two-Phase Interview Process

Remember: Phase One and Phase Two of the interview are distinctly separate. Phase One offers no hint regarding your product or service. It helps you understand the customer without giving away anything about your solution. Phase Two aims to get potential customers' reactions to a solution.

In Phase One, you offer no hint regarding what you may be trying to solve or address. You simply want to get a better sense of what customers are looking for, where they are looking, and how much are they willing to pay. Remember, you have to be very careful not to bring up the subject of price too soon; people might consider such questions pushy, and their guards will go up. Keep it hypothetical. You may ask a question such as, "If something like this existed, at what price point would it be a no-brainer to decide to purchase it?" Keep some emotional distance between you and the solution. It must not look like your particular solution; rather, it should be framed as a possible solution that both you and the people being interviewed are considering and trying to understand. This psychological distinction is very important to maintain in order to keep the process unbiased.

In Phase Two, the conversation is designed to obtain potential customers' reactions to a hypothetical solution. If a product or service appeared that closely resembled your idea, how would

> ### How to Talk to Customers
>
> Be professional. How you communicate is a dominant factor in your relationships with others and determines how successful you will be. Our technology-savvy world makes it tempting to rely exclusively on e-mails and text messages, but communicating with customers face-to-face not only makes a better impression of your product or service but also reaps better data for your market research.
>
> Do not sugarcoat the truth. Communicate honestly with the customer in mind. Rather than comparing and contrasting your product with others on the market, take a collaborative approach when talking to a potential customer. Also make sure you are courteous and polite. Statistics show that being kind and avoiding the "us versus them" approach leads to stronger results and a longer-lasting impression.

they react? Keep in mind during the interview, however, that people often don't know what they want. You must take that reality into account. Still, it's important to hear out your customers.

Talk to lots of people. The more data points you have, the clearer your picture will be. Do not make the mistake of taking any single conversation as gospel. Try to adopt each customer's mindset as you collect data. Always keep in mind the customer to whom you want to sell and why that person would want to buy from you. After conducting five or ten interviews, you'll find your best questioning method. You will then be able to start productive conversations with a wider list of customers.

5.6 How to Get the Conversation Going

How do you break the ice with potential customers? How do you ask these questions? Many techniques are available to get a conversation started. Once you have conducted some interviews with people you know and are comfortable with, you will create your own style. You might even be able to contact somebody by phone or e-mail and say, "Look, I'm doing some important research in the following area. I would like to speak to you for 10 to 15 minutes, and I have 14 questions. Would you be willing to spend a few minutes with me?"

You can say you are an entrepreneur starting a company, or you could pose as someone doing research as a part of a university or organization project. Not everybody will be willing to talk to you, but you will be surprised at how many people *will* be. If you are talking about an area related to their work or something of interest to them, you will find that most people like to have their opinions heard. Finding interviewees will not be as hard as you think.

A few quick thoughts on how to approach your customers with the questions listed above:

1) Allow your interviewee sufficient time to think about each question before responding. Don't hurry anyone.

2) Ask if it would be OK for you to follow up in a couple of months after you have done more research and have more specific ideas. Ask your interviewee, "Would you be willing to participate in shaping this solution further?" Some of your potential customers will want to be part of the process. The answer to this question will also give you an idea of who might be on your customer advisory council, which you should form before going into business.

3) Thank your interviewee at the end of the conversation. At the end of your interview, remember to ask, "Is there any-

thing I should have asked you but forgot?" This question is key; often, people have a lot to say when they hear it.

5.7 How to Find B2B Customers to Talk to

If you are running a business that sells to other businesses (B2B), you will need to find buyers and users in other companies. But how does one start? This question can overwhelm entrepreneurs. I have discovered a number of techniques that work well:

1) **Trade shows.** Trade shows are on the decline, but they still constitute an important place where both competitors and buyers of your products will gather. It is worth going to a trade show, but you will have to be creative. If your budget permits, you may want to get the smallest booth available or share a booth with another small company.

   As I mentioned before, a less expensive method of attending trade shows is to go as an attendee. You will be able to ask questions and learn about your competition through the eyes of your customers. Trade shows also provide opportunities for you to strike up conversations with people who will be your contacts and customers. People grow tired and bored after a day of browsing the aisles and can then be easily engaged in conversation. I have even hired temporary workers to engage in conversations and conduct short surveys with potential customers. I suggest that you strike up conversations and get a sense of the problems people face as well as how they hope to solve them.

2) **Fraternizing.** Find someone who shares common ground with your target customer, for example, an employee in the same company, a student of the same school, and the like. Then get a reference to the target customer through your contact. This tactic makes it easier to build trust and credibility.

3) **Company press releases.** These (usually boring) press releases always contain quotes from prominent individuals in a company. They don't usually devote time to entrepreneurs in person, but they will very likely redirect you to the appropriate individual within the organization. With a reference obtained from an executive-level individual, you can be sure that your lead will work quickly. This technique has worked very well for me in the past.

4) **Mining your social network.** LinkedIn (http://linkedin.com) is probably the most widely used business-related social-networking website. I routinely look there for people who can help me out while I'm doing research. You can find people through your LinkedIn network and ask for 15-minute conversations. People won't always say yes, but if you keep trying, you are bound to get some people to respond.

Through a LinkedIn account, you can connect with professionals around the world, and you can contact people within specific industries. You can potentially reach millions of people through your own direct network, including your friends' friends, their friends' friends, and any additional business acquaintances.

LinkedIn

LinkedIn has over 41 million members in over 200 countries and territories around the world. More than 30% of LinkedIn members use its website for sales and business development. With its vast membership and highly professional users, LinkedIn is a free market-research tool that can connect you with some of the most successful professionals around the world.

Suppose you want to reach somebody who handles advertising focused on food and wine. By typing in just a few key words, you can search for the right people, find them, and make them your business contacts. They may work in public relations departments of companies focused on whatever particular product or service you're interested in. This is how professional social-networking sites such as LinkedIn can boost your market reach and get you acquainted with key people in your industry.

Once you have identified where the market research is needed, you need to work with a social-networking site, such as LinkedIn (or Plaxo at www.Plaxo.com), to get introduced to the appropriate contacts, ask them questions, or request conversations with them. If you follow these techniques, you'll find success. Your success rate, however, will depend on how well you word your questions and on how much effort you put into gaining information.

Ultimately, it's a numbers game. You may have to make 100 attempts to reach 20 people, from whom you will make 10 successful contacts that will lead to 5 useful conversations. The more people you reach out to in a professional, respectful manner, the more productive conversations you will have.

EXAMPLE:
Using LinkedIn to Find People for Market Research

If I needed to find someone with expertise in setting up a call center in Costa Rica, I could start my search as follows:

1) Sign up for a LinkedIn account.
2) Sign in to my account, and click on "Advanced." Under the "Advanced People Search," I would type in the keywords describing the person I'm looking for. It is best to use the words describing the most important criteria of the search, e.g., the type of person, the person's title, the person's location, and the companies the person may have worked for.

For someone who does not have an extensive network, these research results would be weak, but the chances of success increase the more highly connected people one becomes connected to. As I do have an extensive network, my search yields the following:

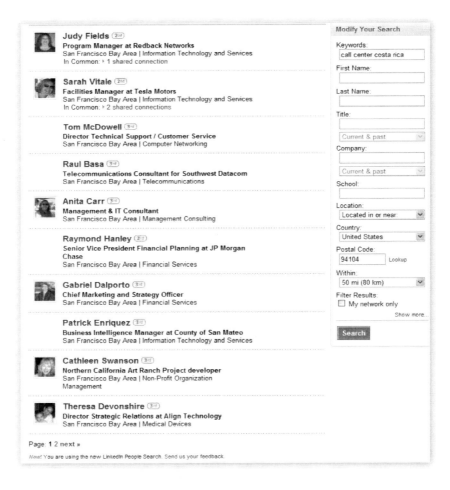

My search for someone to assist in setting up a call center in Costa Rica results in 18 people. The ordinal number after each person's name tells me how far removed they are from me in my network. By using the commands on the page under "Modify Your Search," I can filter my search to find people who are removed from me by no more than two degrees.

As I begin reading the resumes of the people my LinkedIn search recommends, I discover that Theresa was actively involved in setting up call centers in Costa Rica for Align Technology, and, like me, she lives in the San Francisco Bay Area. When I look at the list that tells me how I am connected with Theresa, I see the following:

In order to initiate a request to speak with Theresa, I click on "Get introduced through a connection" and pick Sophia as my immediate connection. Sophia will get an e-mail that asks her to forward a message to Theresa. Voila! If things work out, I'll have a meeting with a prospective subject-matter expert. One of the best parts is the fact that LinkedIn's basic service (which I used here) is free!

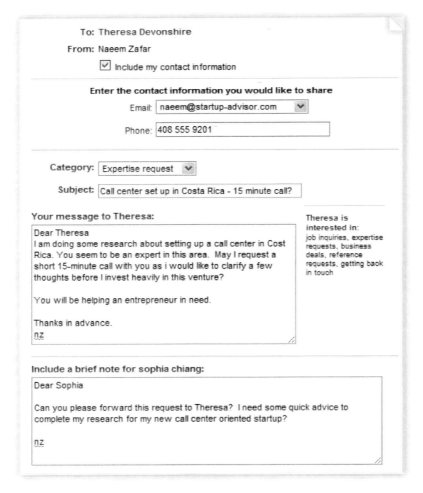

LinkedIn and other social networks, like Go Big Networks, XING, and Facebook, can be powerful tools for finding people who can be part of your market research plans. I use this method extensively.

Create Discussion Groups

Another cool way to find like-minded people on Linkedin and other social networks is to create a discussion group under a specific topic. You will be surprised by how many people will opt-in and join this group. You can start the discussion and others will chime in. This can be a robust place to ask your questions or approach people directly for a more in-depth discussion. Instead of seeking and writing to strangers, you get to talk with people who have opted-in to talk with you.

Last time I checked, there were 88,000 groups formed by people on the LinkedIn network and the top groups had over 200,000 members and several subgroups. It is really easy to start your own group under a very specific topic.

I found 88 groups listed under the heading of "Call Centers."

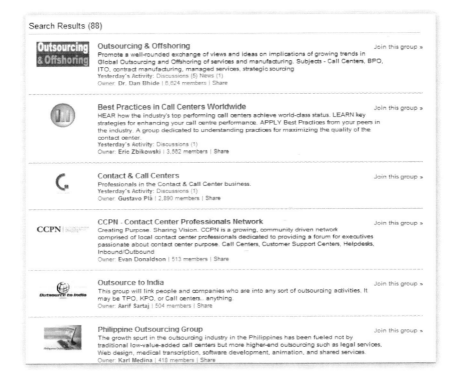

The last posting was about the Philippines specifically, and there was more than one. This is a very powerful ways to connect with people who have a passion about your topic, and they can include subject-matter experts and potential customers.

Chapter 6

Conducting Online Surveys

NOW THAT YOU have found people who can potentially answer a few market research questions for you, you need a third list—a list of people who will take a survey for you on the Internet. These surveys are cheap and easy to develop, and you can find several online survey companies that offer a free account for two weeks. Most of these companies allow you to poll up to 100 people for free. If you pay a small fee—typically $20—you can poll a wider audience. Two of the best-known survey sites are www.surveymonkey.com and www.Zoomerang.com.

The process is simple. Once you create an account, you can watch videos that instruct you on how to create compelling surveys. After you create a short survey, you can do any of the following:

1) Send the survey to a list of people whose e-mail addresses you already have. (Make sure that the people on your list have agreed to receive e-mails from you.)

2) Create a link to the survey and put that link on your website; or create a special website for your survey and drive traffic to that site.

3) Pay the survey company to send your survey to names they provide. Zoomerang claims that they have two million names that have opted to take some surveys. You can use a list of criteria to determine who gets the survey; for example, you may want this survey to go to accountants in California who live in cities with particular attributes.

This last option may be expensive—$5 per completed survey. But in the end, you might be better off spending $200 to $500 on a survey rather than starting down a dead-end street (i.e., a business that not enough people are searching for or care about), only to retreat later with much agony and financial loss.

You can also solicit people from your own alumni networks and local communities and ask them if they would agree to take an online survey. Once they agree, you can send them a link to the survey.

The following is an example of market research that one of my students recently conducted. Viewing the Internet as a great way for kids to connect with other kids across the globe, my student wanted her company to provide international pen pals for children. Seeing such connections as enriching for all kids involved, she wanted to set up a website that would allow young pen pals to connect safely.

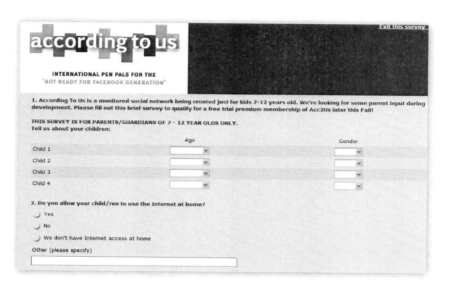

1. According To Us is a monitored social network being created just for kids 7-12 years old. We're looking for some parent input during development. Please fill out this brief survey to qualify for a free trial premium membership of Acc2Us later this Fall!

THIS SURVEY IS FOR PARENTS/GUARDIANS OF 7 - 12 YEAR OLDS ONLY.
Tell us about your children:

	Age	Gender
Child 1		
Child 2		
Child 3		
Child 4		

2. Do you allow your child/ren to use the Internet at home?

- Yes
- No
- We don't have Internet access at home

Other (please specify)

3. On the Acc2Us social network, kids create profile pages to share their everyday lives and make connections with others. What topics or activities would you like your child/ren to do on the site? (check all that apply)

- Hobbies
- Discuss world news/events
- School Life
- Foreign Words
- Practice writing English
- Send messages to other kids
- Games

- Pets
- Jokes
- Earn points to win prizes
- Holidays or special events
- Learn Geography
- Favorite Foods
- Write letters to Pen Pals

- What they do for Fun
- Develop groups of friends
- Where they want to Visit
- Family
- Quizzes

Which one(s) are the most exciting?

4. As premium members (with parental authorization and background security check), kids are invited to create their own profile pages where they can post videos, photos and share their everyday lives with other members around the world. There is no chatting or direct emailing. Internet safety is paramount to the development of Acc2Us. Parents will personally approve any direct communication between PenPals.

Would you be will to pay (subscribe) as a premium member in order for your child/ren to safely communicate with Acc2Us PenPals?

- Yes
- No
- Maybe

Section 2

5. What is the most you would be willing to pay per month (American dollars) for premium membership?

[▾]

In my native currency:

[   ]

6. Do you own a video camera that your child could use to create video content/stories for Acc2Us?

○ Yes

○ No

○ Other (please specify)

[   ]

7. Would you object to small amounts of advertising on the According To Us website?

○ Yes

○ No

8. What do you think is the most important benefit of Acc2Us as described?

○ Something worthwhile online for my kids beyond fantasy or games

○ A safe and fun place for my kids to be online

○ A learning resource

○ Getting exposed to other countries and cultures

○ Other (please describe)

[   ]

9. My level of interest is

○ Definitely interested in having my kid/s joining According To Us!

○ Will decide once I look at the 'live' site

○ Sound good to me, but I don't think my kids would be interested

○ Not interested at all

More comments

[   ]

10. Thank you for your feedback. We will email you a code qualifying you for a free trial premium membership to According To Us within 60 days:

First Name [   ]

Last Name [   ]

City/Town: [   ]

State/Province: [   ]

Country: [   ]

Email Address: [   ]

[Done]

Above is the simple survey she created first to learn what parents would want in such a site. You may create a survey with even more simple or more creative questions. I am only using this example to illustrate the method and am not suggesting that these are the best questions for you to use in your survey.

The results of the survey are automatically tabulated, and they come out looking like this:

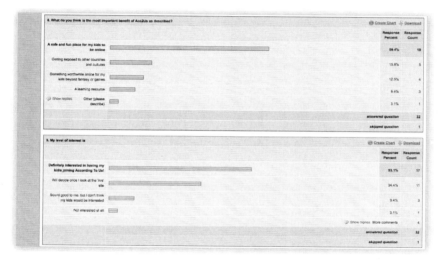

These survey findings provided the following information:

1) They helped determine the threshold for pricing.

2) They showed which features parents thought their kids would like the best. (Of course, surveying and testing with kids themselves would be more helpful in determining what they would like.)

3) They provided feedback regarding advertisements on the site.

4) They revealed what parents saw as the most important benefits of such a site.

Another productive technique for attracting people to answer your questions is to drive traffic to your webpage using Google AdWords. I explain how to do this in the next chapter.

Simple Tips to Remember about Online Surveys

One has to clearly understand what he or she wants to get out of the survey and structure the questions accordingly. If I go to a customer with an online survey question saying, "I'm thinking about this cool feature, would it be useful?" and provide "yes," "no," and "maybe" as possible answers, more than likely, the response will be "maybe"; and if it is, the data is useless to me. Maybe a better way to go about this is to rephrase the question assessing the usefulness of the feature by mapping it according to willingness to pay.

The survey questions should be well structured and sequential with one question leading to another. The survey should be circulated among a diverse group of people. Otherwise, the results obtained could be skewed, and the interpretation drawn from such data could lead to false assumptions.

Chapter 7

Using Google AdWords to Conduct Market Research

BEFORE YOU BEGIN to develop your product and market it to the world, you must be sure you have sufficient knowledge of your market.

Starting up a company is a time-consuming endeavor. Many entrepreneurs rush into the development phase of their product or service prematurely. They believe that their product or service is a brilliant idea, but when they get their product to market, they realize that this seemingly "brilliant" idea was not what consumers wanted. Unfortunately, this premature development happens more often than you would believe. By following this guide, you can potentially avoid this fate.

I will outline an important technique that will help you correctly gauge your market. It utilizes services provided by Google in order to create a survey website, advertise this site, and then analyze the results.

The main questions that you are trying to answer using Google are the following:

1) What things are people searching for, and what keywords are likely to generate more interest?
(This can help shape your product ideas.)

2) How many people are interested in particular topics or products, and can you interest them in your offering?

3) What is your competition likely to be selling to your audience?

4) What will be the customer acquisition cost if you decide to use online advertising for your product or service before creating it?

5) Can you drive some traffic to your online survey in order to collect additional information about your customers and possibly engage them in a conversation?

Google provides great services for an entrepreneur looking to measure a particular consumer base, and one of the most important ways to gauge your market is through a survey. As discussed above, there are many ways to do this. If you were planning to market a coffee-related product, for example, you could simply go to a coffee shop and ask people about their tastes and preferences. But, in our Internet-savvy world, there is a much better way to learn about your audience.

In this section, I outline a three-step method that will allow you to validate whether people are interested in the product or service that you are about to develop. By following this method, you will see if your business is viable.

Here is a brief overview of the three-step method:

1) You set up a simple one- or two-page website, or landing page, on www.sites.google.com. Using Google Sites, it will take you 30 minutes or less to set up a landing page that describes your product or service. Make sure it describes who you are and why you are conducting this market research, and ensure that it has a contact e-mail address. You can ask a few questions right there, or, better yet, you can tell your visitors what you are researching and ask them to answer a few questions by clicking a link to your survey on www.Zoomerang.com or www.SurveyMonkey.com. There are videos on these sites that teach you how to create a good survey and how to create a link from your existing website or the landing page that you just created.

2) Using Google AdWords (www.adwords.google.com), make at least three ads that contain catchy descriptions of your product or service and a link to the landing page you created with Google Sites.

3) Using Google Analytics and the data provided in Google AdWords, analyze the data on how many people clicked on your ad and what they had to say by looking at their sur-

vey answers. You are doing this to see whether or not your business is viable.

In the example I used in the last chapter, the entrepreneur started by setting up a landing page. This simple one-page website, shown below, provides some basic information and directs its readers to take a short survey.

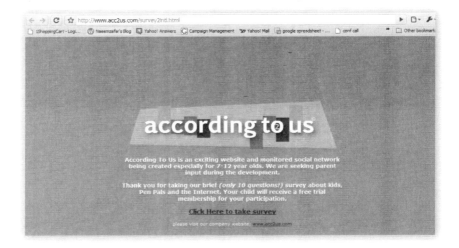

This site is extremely simple. It just explains its purpose and asks people to take a short survey. Nevertheless, it is a great way to be able to get a feel for the market. The question remains, however, how did this person drive the traffic to her website? This is where Google AdWords comes in. A few years ago, this software cost over $10,000, but now it's almost free. And it should be a major part of analyzing what your customers want.

Basically, my student set up her AdWords account at www.ad-words.google.com.

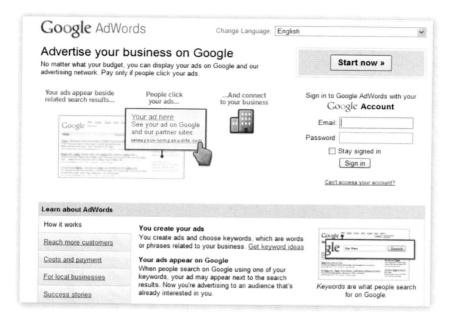

The site contains all the necessary instructions for setting up your own ads—something that's easy to learn if you just spend one hour reading through the site. It takes $5 to set up an account, and then the site allows you to create short, four-line Google links. You pay based only on how many people actually click on your ad, but you can set up how much you're willing to spend per day. You also choose where and how often your ad will be displayed.

Here is how my student created her ad with Google AdWords:

Create ad group

Name this ad group

An ad group should focus on one product or service. Each ad group can contain one or more ads and a keywords, placements, or both.

Ad group name: `Ad Group #1`

Create an ad

Enter your first ad here. You can create more ads later. Help me write an effective text ad.

To create another ad type save your incomplete ad group, then go to the "Ads" tab to create your ad.

Headline	Safe Pen Pals for Kids
Description line 1	Survey for Parents of 6-12 yr olds
Description line 2	Free Premium Membership
Display URL	www.acc2us.com
Destination URL	http:// ▾ www.acc2us.com

Ad preview

Safe Pen Pals for Kids
Survey for Parents of 6-12 yr olds
Free Premium Membership
www.acc2us.com

Once you create your ad (Don't worry! It won't start until you tell it to start.), you create a list of "keywords." Keywords are the phrases that are typed into the search window by someone using Google to search for something online. Whenever people search on Google using keywords that you have placed a bid on, your ad will be shown in the "Sponsored Link" section of the Google search results page to compete in real time with other people's ads.

Just to clarify, if you were to do a search on Google for "pen pals," this is what you could find:

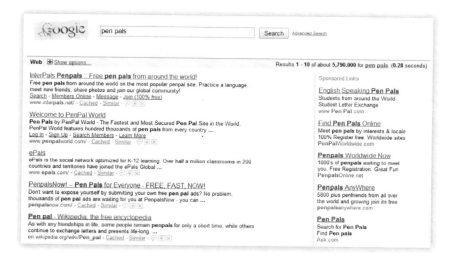

The results in the left column are known as organic search results. The column on the right side is for "Sponsored Links." (You could also find sponsored links in the top few slots on the left side. They would be marked with a colored background and also labeled "Sponsored Links.") This is what it looks like when you buy a keyword and your ad is displayed in response to a search using that word. In this example, "pen pals" is the keyword that was both bid on as well as searched. There were many other keywords bid on, too.

As you can see from the full list below, it is good to try various combinations of words, singulars and plurals, and some misspellings as well. You never know how someone will type their search.

(Remember: Putting a series of words in quotes asserts that an exact match be found.)

Section 2

Google Analytics

One of the nicest things about Google is that it provides good analytics. Once you start your ad campaign, it will tell you how many times an ad was displayed (the number of "impressions"), how many times somebody clicked on your ad and you paid for it (the "CTR," or Click Through Rate), the average cost per click ("CPC"), and the average position in the list where your ad was shown. Positions one through three in the ad list are usually the most expensive. If the number for the average position is greater than eight, then your ad was not served on the first page of the Google results. That is not good as most people never click on the second page of Google results. In this case, you may want to improve your ad position by increasing your maximum bid.

Full List of Keywords:

"e-mail pals"

free pen pals for kids

international pen pals

international pen pals for kids

international pen pals kids

international penpals for kids

kid penpals

kids pen pal

kids pen pals

kids penpals

pen friends

pen pal for kids

pen pals for children

pen pals for kids

penpal for kids

penpals for kids

social network for tweens

girls 9-12

parenting tweens

kids Online

tweens

pre teens

pre-teens

pre-teens online

preteens

preteens websites

penpals kids

Remember that you only pay Google if somebody actually clicks on your ad and ends up on your landing page. Furthermore, you can set daily limits on how much are you willing to spend. Google keeps track of these limits and will stop showing your ad after you have exhausted your daily maximum.

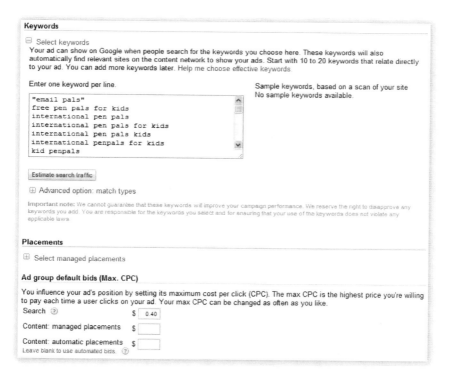

You can also ask Google to estimate the amount of traffic you can expect, given your set of keywords, and what the resulting cost should be (see example below). Personally, I think Google is generally too optimistic with its estimates, so I use numbers smaller than what it suggests.

Section 2

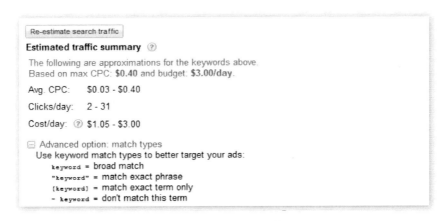

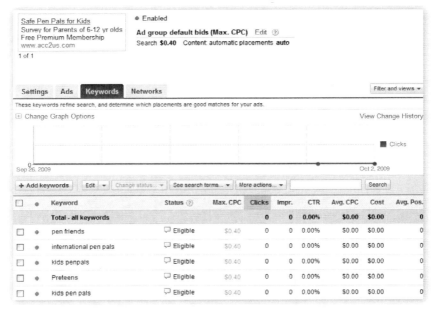

The analytics revealed after one week of running the "pen pals" ad were as follows:

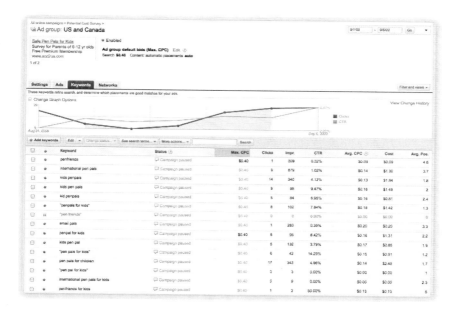

This page shows results based on how well each keyword performed, e.g., for "penfriends," our ad was displayed 309 times but got only one click. The keyword "kids penpals" had 14 clicks for 340 impressions and a CTR of 4.12%. The keyword performing second best was "pen pals for kids." It got 6 clicks in 42 displays and had a CTR of 14.29%, for a total cost of 91 cents. It had an average display position of 1.2—not bad for some low-cost market research.

How Google AdWords works

Google conducts an auction in real time as your search results are being tabulated. This means that even if I bid a maximum of 40 cents per click, I may pay only 3 cents or 11 cents for each click if no one else is bidding on those keywords at that time. If the word is hot and people are willing to pay 50 cents for their ads to be displayed in top spots, I will lose out on this auction and my ad will not be shown. Oh well, I must control the cost of my market research.

Key Message:

Before you spend tons of time developing your product or service, use the keyword searches of Google AdWords to discover how many people are searching for just such a solution to meet their needs. This research can be enlightening, and it can give you the opportunity to ask the people who respond to your ads to take a survey or simply write to you so you can start a conversation with them. What better way to find customers than to communicate with people who are searching for a solution that you plan to offer.

Chapter 8

Using Twitter to Do Market Research

MOST PEOPLE THINK of Twitter as a waste of time, but they have yet to realize the potential of this wonderful tool that is transforming our Internet usage. For those of you who do not yet know what Twitter (www.Twitter.com) is, it is a free means of following people who interest you. Furthermore, anyone with a Twitter account can publicly broadcast short messages of up to 140 characters that can be received in your web browser or on your mobile device as an SMS. This seemingly simple technique is transforming how people communicate, how businesses build communities, and how politicians get their messages out instantaneously. (You can follow the author of this work by simply going to www.Twitter.com/naeem and clicking "Follow" once you have created your own Twitter account.)

Twitter provides us with an instant look at what is happening in the world right now. It is real time. What you need to learn is how you can use Twitter to do your market research.

8.1 How to do Market Research on Twitter

The most powerful feature on Twitter is the "Search" button. It is your window to what people are talking about. Let's say you want to start a business that serves as a market place for programs that help high school students studying for their SATs, the Scholastic Aptitude Tests used to help place students into colleges in the United States. You want to talk with few people as a part of your market research. This is how you may use Twitter to perform this research:

(Once you are signed in, you may not see the search box, so start at www.Twitter.com and do not sign in.)

In the search box, type "about SAT prep," and see what you get.

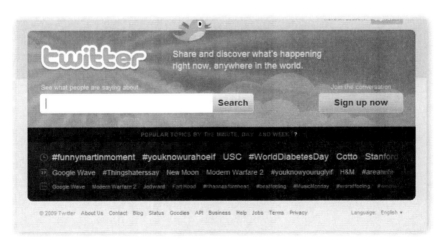

SAT prep | **Search**

Realtime results for **SAT prep**

kassieee Whoa. My **SAT prep** math class is actually paying off. My grade has increased by 120 points since the first practice test. :O
7 minutes ago from Echofon

raerunsfast @erriicababy Yeah. I had **SAT prep** class today. LAME. Then I hung out at my mom's shop for a while.
13 minutes ago from web

MyLifeIsActing @CuteMileyRay boring **SAT Prep**....ehh lol nd i actually cried when i saw a miley vid of her going on stage cuz i wnt 2 go 2 her concert! :D
27 minutes ago from web

_kristincar **sat** and act **prep**... wow i have some life
about 1 hour ago from txt

zhenren 演出后女儿去朋友家cast party 可能没睡觉了。明天下午她必须开始 **SAT prep** 课程。我在1977有很完地约会也睡得很小早上上GRE超过600。够了进去johns Hopkins 研究学院。
about 2 hours ago from Tweetie

ohnolisa @Courtt_Whoaa I'm a junior. I still have time, but my **SAT prep** class is making me look :P
about 2 hours ago from web

Apparently many people are having trouble with SAT preparation. We notice that kassieee is indeed preparing for her SAT and doing well. If you search further down, you will notice that several people are, in fact, interested in preparing for their SATs.

You can note their screen names, do a search in Twitter, and chose to follow them. If they also follow you, then you will be able to send them a direct message. This message will only go to the person you are sending it to and not to everyone who showed up in your search. Tweetdeck (www.Tweetdeck.com) can be downloaded for free and used as the program for sending messages. Using Tweetdeck, you can send Kassieee a direct message:

Although you may have a low rate of success, some people will reply to your messages and will be willing to engage in a dialog with you. You know that they are interested in the topic at hand, and you may be able to direct them to your online survey or simply talk with them to validate your market research.

A real-time search on Twitter can be a very powerful tool for market research.

8.2 How to Get Specific in Your Search

Twitter search has a few options that allow you to be more specific. You can use an operator such as "OR" or "AND" to combine words, and you can use a minus sign to eliminate words; for example, in the search described above, the following changes can be made to produce more specific results:

By adding a minus sign before a word, you can eliminate that word from the tweets that are found. Adding the word "OR," in capital letters, between two words will cause Twitter to search for results containing either of these words.

In the picture below, I repeat the search, but this time I do not want to see tweets about Saturday (so "Sat" for Saturday won't be confused with the "SAT" exam), and I also do not want to see any tweets that use the word "prep." I am trying to eliminate tweets where people may be talking about preparing for a Saturday night out on the town.

You can also zoom in and narrow your search to people located near you. This would allow you to connect with these local people and to have an opportunity to sell your product to them as well. By narrowing down the area of focus, you can get very specific and can find people who may be interested in having a conversation for the sake of your market research. While this technique may not work for everyone, I find it to be a powerful tool that all entrepreneurs must consider. It may actually be easier than trying to find a few people to talk to at your local coffee shop!

Chapter 9

Publicly Available Data for Free Market Research

9.1 Other Resources You Can Use

There are a number of other online resources besides the ones discussed above that can be used for market research; and you will be amazed to find out how much market data is indeed available for free. In this chapter, I will give you a few more tips and ideas to help you access these resources. I will introduce you to sites like www.census.gov where you can get information that will help you size your target market and give you some clarity regarding where to start positioning your product. The Securities and Exchange Commission's site, www.SEC.gov, will be a great source of free information about specific markets, including market dynamics and size as well as growth histories of individual companies. This information will help create "proxies," or examples that will help justify the assumptions you must make for your own startup. It is a lot more convincing to say that your company will reach 100,000 users in two years if you can provide three proxies of

Public vs. Private Companies

All companies are either privately held, with stocks unavailable for purchase unless specifically sold by the company, or public, where shares can be bought on a stock exchange, through a broker, or online. A company has to have substantial revenues and be well established before it can "go public" and get lawyers and investment brokers involved. A startup is far from being in that position, but that is the goal of most entrepreneurs. Going public is an affirmation that a business has taken off and the Security and Exchange Commission (SEC) will allow it to sell its shares to ordinary citizens. It is also the time when you can convert your personal ownership into wealth by selling your own shares on the open market. In order to reach this point, a company must comply with a long list of requirements from SEC know as an Initial Public Offering, or IPO.

other companies with similar offerings or demographic focuses who achieved similar penetration in the past.

Why do you need to look at public companies? Remember, most public companies were once small startup companies, like yours. In their initial public offering (IPO) filing documents, they each had to provide a complete data report, including surveys and other types of research. These reports are great sources of information for your new business. My favorite of these reports is called an S1 filing.

Suppose your business is in healthcare and you need to solve a problem you have with delivery and your supply chain. As you search for a solution to your problem, it would be helpful for you to research the last five companies that went public in your sector or domain and see how they dealt with similar problems. You can find such information easily by using the Internet and doing a Google search, and it shouldn't take you more than half an hour.

IPO VIEW-Outlook for healthcare IPOs improving

* Healthcare IPOs saw mixed 2009

Fri Dec 25, 2009 12:16am EST

STOCKS | IPOS | HEALTHCARE

Stocks

* Investors friendlier to healthcare IPOs in 2010

Omeros Corporation
OMER.O
$5.61
▲ +0.02 ▲ +0.36%
12:00am PST

* Obama healthcare plan seen helping

By Clare Baldwin

NEW YORK, Dec 25 (Reuters) - Healthcare companies are lining up to go public, and they could get a warmer reception in 2010 as investors' risk appetite increases, and new legislation potentially leads to more profit for the sector.

Concord Medical
Services Holdings
Limited
CCM.N
$8.56
▼ -0.04 ▼ -0.47%
12:00am PST

The U.S. Senate on Thursday approved President Barack Obama's healthcare reform bill. It must negotiate with the House of Representatives over a final version, but if the bill passes, it would provide additional money to healthcare companies.

Talecris
biotherapeutics
holdings corp.
TLCR.O
$21.42
▼ -0.14 ▼ -0.65%
12:00am PST

New legislation won't immediately translate into more healthcare IPOs, experts cautioned, but added it would generally boost the sector, and the pipeline looks healthy.

"It will be 3 to 5 years before you start seeing significant uptick in the number of companies that are coming to the public market due to the Obama healthcare plan," said Benjamin Howe, Chief Executive at investment bank America's Growth Capital.

Still, a recovering economy and hopes of money in a few years could be helping companies go public now.

When I did a quick search, I found an article on the first page of results that gives me data about three companies that recently went public. A few more clicks revealed blogs and data about other public companies.

For financial information on the specific market you need to research, you can also go to websites like www.Finance.Yahoo.com, Google Financials, and www.Schwab.com. Websites such as these provide information on specific companies that have gone public. Once you have identified the companies that have gone public in your area, a site like www.SeekingAlpha.com can put together all of the data in one place.

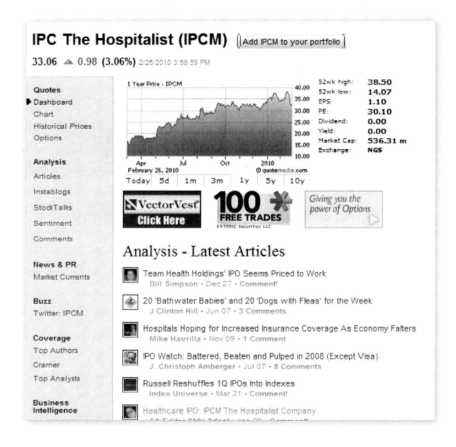

www.seekingalpha.com

As you can see, you can get to a company's SEC filing—this is where the most useful S1 document is available—as well as the market analysis, a discussion of competition, and its financial statements.

9.2 Hire People to Do Market Research for You

Should you decide to hire people to do your market research for you, you can use free sources like www.craigslist.com, www.elance. com, www.odesk.com, and www.guru.com as resources for finding people to hire. People in the United States, as well as overseas, can very efficiently do market research on your behalf, and it will only cost you a few dollars per hour. Thus, for a $100 or $150 investment, you can get extensive market research about the companies in your focus area of interest—information such as who they are, what are their addresses, and what are the names of potential contacts in those companies. Especially by using research assistants who live in emerging economies, you can find free or affordable resources available to you for your market research.

Use the Internet, Extensively!

We are privileged to live at a time when we have the world at our fingertips thanks to the Internet. Thanks to this efficient tool, market research has never been easier. Whether it is by using LinkedIn to make contacts or checking company reports on the Securities and Exchange Commission website (www.SEC.gov), entrepreneurs can easily access a plethora of information for free.

9.3 Using Free Data from Trade Associations

An industry trade group, also known as a trade association, is an organization founded and funded by businesses that operate in a specific industry. An industry trade association participates in public relations activities such as advertising, education, political donations, lobbying, and publishing, but its main focus is collaboration between companies, or standardization.

Guess how these associations, which are supported by member committees, manage to stay in business? By sending free information to anyone who asks for it! That will be YOU!

There is nobody who will be more excited to hear from you and have you ask for all kinds of data. This is what they do—all day long. They are judged by how much information they disseminate to inquiring minds such as yours. You are the one who is looking for free information on an industry, such as the names and products of its key players, and trying to understand its market dynamics; thus, by contacting a trade association for such information, you hit the jackpot. Nothing pleases the director of a trade association more than being able to send out a packet of free information, but I find that many entrepreneurs do not use these resources at all. There are thousands of such organizations throughout the world, especially in the U.S. You can find them at the following website (or through your favorite search engine on the Internet): http://www.google.com/Top/Business/Associations/By_Industry/

When you use this link, it will bring you to a list of dozens of trade organizations, sorted by industry.

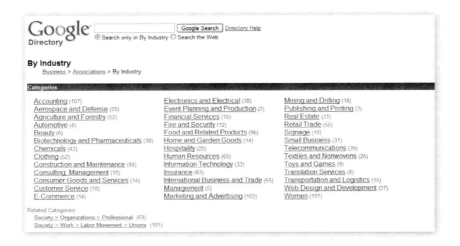

Click on the industry that you are searching for, and you will see something like this:

The screen above resulted from clicking on the "Food and Related Products" link. There are 96 trade associations sorted into 9 categories such as "Beverages," "Dairy," and "Produce."

If you were interested in learning more about the beverage industry for your startup, you would click on one of the names mentioned on the site above. This would take you to the American Beverage Association Website (see below). With this information, you would quickly be able to find the names and numbers of companies in this industry. Suppose you're looking to talk with some companies that make flavors for drinks. Voila! They are all listed as members on this site. I can now make contact with, seek information from, and even talk to someone at any of those companies.

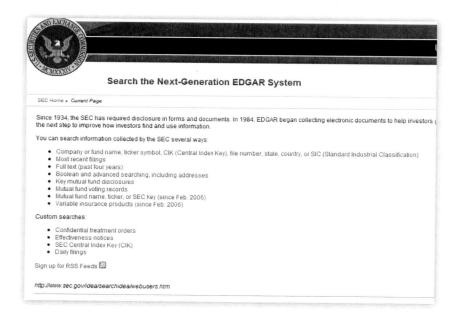

If you planned to do a startup in the area of gluten-free candy bars and were looking for the market size of major companies in the Dry Pea and Lentil Counsil, a few clicks would get you this contact information:

Contact Us

The USA Dry Pea & Lentil Council hopes that this site is informative and also user-friendly.

USA Dry Pea & Lentil Council
2780 W. Pullman Road
Moscow,
Phone: (208) 882-3023
Fax: (208) 882-6406
pulse@pea-lentil.com

9.4 More Free Research Using Data on Public Companies:

SEC and Edgar.com

Prior to embarking on any business idea, it is very important to perform extensive market research to validate that idea. Aside from talking to and surveying as many people as you can, Security and Exchange Commission (SEC) filings can be a great resource for learning about different industries, trends, companies, and products. SEC is a governmental organization that regulates companies who are public (i.e., can sell shares to anyone through a stock exchange). In order to protect the consumer, there are heavy requirements for compliance and all companies have to file detailed documents quarterly, annually, and whenever they have any significant event.

The SEC website, www.SEC.gov, is for U.S.-based companies, but just about every country has an equivalent organization that regulates public companies in that country.

Every publicly traded company in the United States must file a series of reports with the SEC. Below is a brief summary of the reports that you might find helpful when performing your market research:

1) **10-K:** Each publicly traded company is required to file a 10-K report to the SEC within 60 days after the end of its fiscal year. These comprehensive reports contain extensive company overviews, details on the competitive landscapes, key strategies and risks of the year, company histories, descriptions of organizational structures, and much more.[1] I find the following sections of the 10-K very helpful:

   a) *Business*—This section contains a very specific description of the company, its products and services, its subsidiaries, and the markets in which it operates. Additionally, some companies include details on their recent events, competition, regulations, labor issues, special operating costs, seasonal factors, and insurance matters.

---

1   See http://www.investopedia.com/terms/1/10-k.asp.

b) *Risk Factors*—This is the explanation of what keeps the executive team up at night. It is in this section that the company explains everything that could go wrong, such as potential failures to meet obligations, and the likely external effects. The purpose of this section is to make sure current investors and potential investors are adequately warned about problems that could arise.

c) *Properties*—This section provides a description of each company's significant properties, including its physical assets and its intellectual property.

Thomson Research

Thomson Research is yet another resource available to entrepreneurs. Thomson Research tracks all SEC filings and provides company and market research reports. It provides company financials, earning estimates, and news—information entrepreneurs can use to gauge the success of the companies in their own industries and to watch trends develop.

d) *Legal Proceedings*—This is where one will find a company's disclosure of any significant pending lawsuits or other legal proceedings.

e) *Market for Registrant's Common Equity and Related Stockholder Matters*—This simple statement gives the highs and lows of company stock.

f) *Management's Discussion and Analysis*—This detailed description of a company's operations compares the current period to the prior period. These comparisons provide an overview of the operational issues that could cause increases or decreases in business.[2]

---

2   See http://en.wikipedia.org/wiki/Form_10-K#Item_1_-_Business.

2) **8-K:** This is the company's disclosure of significant un-
scheduled events that would be of interest to its shareholders and to the SEC. These reports must be filed within four
business days after the event occurs. The most common
reasons for filing an 8-K include the following:

a) Changes in control of registrant

b) Acquisition or disposition of assets

c) Bankruptcy or receivership

d) Changes in registrant's certifying accountant

e) Resignations of registrant's directors

f) Financial statements and exhibits

g) Changes in fiscal year

h) Regulation fd disclosure

i) Amendments to the registrant's code of ethics or waiver
of a provision of the code of ethics

j) Public notice of pension fund blackout period

k) Public release of nonpublic information regarding results of operations or financial condition for a completed quarterly or annual fiscal period

3) **S-1:** A requirement for companies that intend to go public and list their stock on a national exchange, this filing requires the following descriptions from each company:

a) Plan for use of proceeds from the capital raised

b) Business model

c) Competitors

d) Planned security prospectus

e) Offering-price methodology

f) Possible dilutions to other listed securities

The SEC also requires the disclosure of any material business dealings between the company and its directors and outside counsel.

4) **20-F:** This annual report of foreign private issuers must be filed within the next six months after the end of a company's fiscal year. Its purpose is to standardize the reporting requirements of foreign-based companies so that investors can evaluate these investments alongside domestic equities.

Favorite Filing

I never thought that I would confess my love for an SEC filing, but I think that S-1 filings are great. I love S-1 filings, otherwise known as the prospectus that is filed when a company attempts to go public. As these companies must disclose everything about their businesses to shareholders, their S-1s are full of useful data for entrepreneurs. I read and even collect them!

There is a great deal of information available, but it can be very time consuming to manually read through individual SEC filings. If you're interested in researching a particular topic rather than specific companies or if you don't know how to find the exact information you need, it would be impractical for you to read through entire filings to find the specific information that you're looking for. In situations like these, online tools such as 10-K Wizard, EdgarOnline, and Accounting Research Manager's (ARM) 10-K Lookup can be very helpful.

This is the page from www.SEC.gov, the official site of the Security and Exchange Commission and access point to EDGAR:

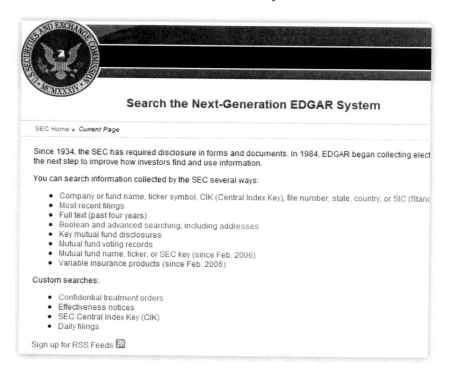

Search the Next-Generation EDGAR System

SEC Home » *Current Page*

Since 1934, the SEC has required disclosure in forms and documents. In 1984, EDGAR began collecting elect the next step to improve how investors find and use information.

You can search information collected by the SEC several ways:

- Company or fund name, ticker symbol, CIK (Central Index Key), file number, state, country, or SIC (Stand
- Most recent filings
- Full text (past four years)
- Boolean and advanced searching, including addresses
- Key mutual fund disclosures
- Mutual fund voting records
- Mutual fund name, ticker, or SEC key (since Feb. 2006)
- Variable insurance products (since Feb. 2006)

Custom searches:

- Confidential treatment orders
- Effectiveness notices
- SEC Central Index Key (CIK)
- Daily filings

Sign up for RSS Feeds

EDGAR stands for Electronic Data Gathering, Analysis, and Retrieval, This database was implemented by the SEC to do two things: 1) to quickly process time-sensitive information of publicly held companies, and 2) to provide investors with easier access to company information.

EDGAR became available to filers on July 15, 1992. As of May 6, 1996, all domestic publicly held companies were required to submit financial information via EDGAR.

Researching Public Companies Through EDGAR: A Guide for Investors

The SEC's EDGAR database provides free public access to corporate information, allowing you to quickly research a company's financial information and operations by reviewing registration statements, prospectuses and periodic reports filed on Forms 10-K and 10-Q. You als can find information about recent corporate events reported on Form 8- but that a company does not have to disclose to investors.

EDGAR also provides access to comment and response letters relating to disclosure filings made after August 1, 2004, and reviewed by either the Division of Corporation Finance or the Division of Investment Managemer On May 22, 2006, the staffs of the Divisions of Corporation Finance and Investment Management began to use the EDGAR system to issue notifications of effectiveness for Securities Act registration statements : post-effective amendments, other than those that become effective automatically by law. These notifications will be posted to the EDGAR system the morning after a filing is determined to be effective.

Finding market analysis and financial data for companies in your domain

Once you find out when a particular company went public, you can go to the SEC website and click on the EDGAR link to go through the company filing and look for the initial public offering prospectus. This prospectus is a very rich source of information, citing all kinds of market data and other resources of information. You are free to use this information—since it is publicly disclosed—as long as you cite its source.

This research should be done as part of your own thinking process and business-plan development. When researching each company on EDGAR, you should look for the following:

1) Market dynamics information
2) Competitive landscape information
3) Information on pricing and revenue in the early years
4) Market trends information

All this data is free, and it can help you develop your ideas regarding what your startup may do in situations similar to those experienced by the companies you research. It can also help you learn who you should be wary of and who you could possibly partner with.

How to Use 10-K Wizard to Conduct Market Research

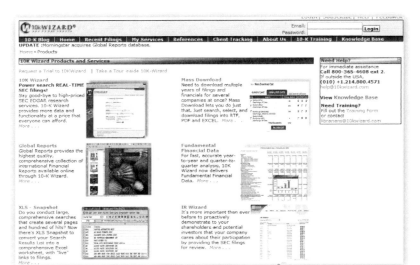

The search engine 10-K Wizard at www.10KWizard.com is a subsidiary of Morningstar that allows users to focus their company searches on particular areas. This helps you find the results you need and significantly reduces your research time. When you use 10-K Wizard, you can quickly find answers within financial filings or search for specific language within sections of all SEC filings. It is not a free service, however, with the basic package costing upwards of $300; but this package includes an annual subscription, and there is a five-day free trial to test out the site before making your purchase. Its users are able to customize their searches through a variety of different criteria such as date, industry, revenues, ticker, company name, keywords, and much more. Additionally, users can specify the type of filing that they want to focus their search on.

Imagine starting a company that makes iPhone applications. A good place to start your research might be reviewing Apple's 10-K filing. This would allow you to learn the size of the iPhone market, the number of existing applications, and who is actually using these applications.

If you're interested in finding more information about Apple's third-party applications data and you decide to review its most recent 10-K filing, once the filing is selected, you will see a table of contents like the one shown below. If you're planning on making an iPhone and an iPod Touch application, you would be interested in the current sales of the two devices, as well as their performance, as compared to previous quarters. The first step would be to look up the "Net Sales" portion of the filing.

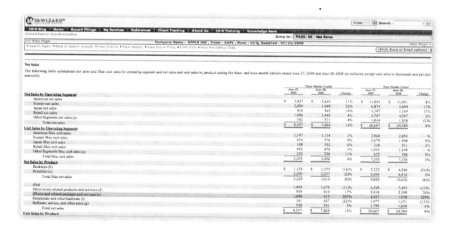

From the above data, you can see that at the end of the nine-month period, iPhone sales skyrocketed 303% from $1,038 to $4,457. iPod net sales decreased by 13%. Overall, these net sales

Section 2

amounts show that the demand for both the iPhone and the iPod Touch are strong and that the market for these products is growing at an exponential rate.

The second page of the Net Sales page gives a qualitative explanation of Apple's financial results:

As shown on this page, iPhone handset sales totalled 13.4 million during the first nine months of 2009, and unit sales of the iPhone increased by 4.5 million units or 626%.

According to this page,

> Net sales of other music-related products and services increased $139 million or 17% and $510 million or 20% during the third quarter of 2009 and first nine months of 2009, respectively, compared to the same periods in 2008.

From just 10 minutes on the 10-K Wizard website, you now have more information to help determine the validity of a new third-party application for iPhone and iPod Touch. With the continued demand for iPhones and the surge of iTunes profits due to third-party applications, there might be a viable market. I have provided more examples using other resources in Appendix 2 (available as a separate document). Please refer to that section to learn even more about this method of market research.

Conclusion

There is an enormous amount of information available to you for free. You should think about supplementing your primary research with this additional data in order to create a solid understanding of the market, including its size and its dynamics. This is what your investors expect you to know.

Disclaimer:

I realize that this method of research is not always applicable to every entrepreneur. Depending on the country you live in and the type of business you are starting, the methods will change, but I wanted to show you what is possible on the Internet. Please apply these processes to discover a deeper understanding of your own market before you embark on the long journey of starting your own business.

Section 3
Extracting Meaning from Market Research

OK, now that you have talked to customers and users, conducted online surveys, spent time on Google AdWords, and finished looking at the publicly available data on related companies, what should you do next? Well, now it's time to put together all the information you have gathered. This is the time to extract those four main diagrams that we talked about early on.

I have always wondered how people know that they're done with their market research, because the fact of the matter is you're never done. Just the same, if you can draw these four diagrams and discuss them without hesitation, then you are done enough to go on to the next task.

I showed you these four diagrams earlier. In the next four chapters, I will provide you with additional thoughts as to how you can create these diagrams for your own business.

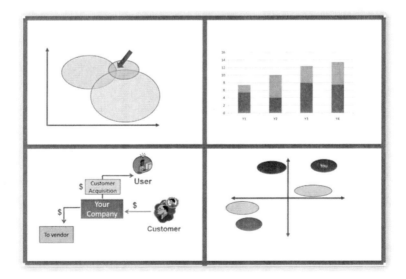

Chapter 10

Profiling Your Target Customers

THIS IS PROBABLY the most important diagram for you to draw; but entrepreneurs seem to have a lot of difficulty with this one.

Imagine that the blue pie below represents all the people who can use your product or service. I realize that everyone on earth would benefit from your product or service, but you have to ask who needs it more than anyone else. Entrepreneurs often get stuck here. They see such a large market for their product, yet their marketing budget is so small that they can't even begin to reach everybody. The solution is simple: find a sliver of the market, a subset that really needs your product more than anyone else.

For example, let's say your product is a platform that can connect students who need tutoring help with people who can provide it for a fee, such as professors and teachers. The students, and the tutors, can be located anywhere in the world. This is an exciting idea, and it is bound to take off someday.

Looking at the picture above, who is in the blue section of your pie? Every student, anywhere on the planet! Yes, that is true, but let's take a minute to segment this market. Ask yourself where you'll find the teachers and how you'll attract the right type of students. If you did your market research in Section 2, it should have told you that the students who have the most problems are high school students working on physics and math.

Your interviews with prospective students and additional research should have provided you with some clarity about not only which subjects students need help with but also how much they are willing to spend to get this help.

Start with a Sliver and Own it, Then You Can Expand

Continuing to use the above example, you might focus your tutoring service on just one or two subjects initially, such as math and physics, and start the service in just one city or school district. You could find out which books are being used in the schools, and you could recruit teachers, or students who have already graduated, as tutors. Your research takes out many variables and allows you to focus on one segment of the total market. The problem that most entrepreneurs encounter is dilution of focus, resources, and funds. Although your service can be used with multiple subjects in multiple cities, you should pick one and see if you can make that subsegment successful first. There are multiple moving parts in any business, and you must simplify and minimize these moving parts in order to assure success.

Whatever you do, you need to understand that once you manage to provide tutoring in your school district for a few hundred students, it will be easy to reach out to other math and physics students in your state or province. Once you have conquered a vast number of physics and math tutors and students, then you can think about adding new subjects, new geographies, or other ways of expanding the pie.

But puhleeeez start with a small sliver that you can conquer. Most entrepreneurs cannot see themselves "limiting" themselves in this way. Their ideas remain bloated and, thus, never take off. You really have to rethink segmentation. Segmentation is about identifying the people who need you most and then validating that assumption through market research. Then, you can put all of the wood behind your arrow to make sure that you can serve this segment really well. You have limited energy, limited resources, and dozens of other moving parts to address. You are in no position to launch a multicity, multiproduct startup. That will come over time as you gain knowledge, experience, finances, and traction. Traction is the most important aspect of market validation and shows that people like what you have to offer and are willing to spend money to buy it.

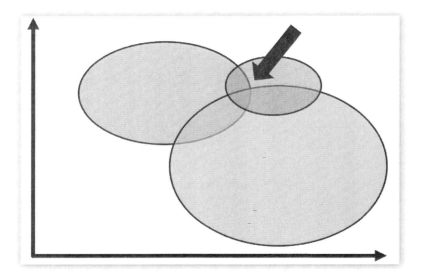

In the diagram above, you can draw your own target segment. We had considered this example before when a startup was targeting students who needed help with college preparation exams in certain subjects. The big, pink bubble represents high school students applying to college or a university. The top left (gray) bubble represents all students struggling with physics and advanced math. The small blue bubble represents students who shop online or have a credit card and, thus, can purchase your service on demand.

The intersection of these three circles is that little triangle and that represents your **target segment**: Students who are applying to a college, are struggling with physics or math in high school, and have the ability to make a purchase decision in case they need help improving their test scores.

This example is for illustration purposes only. The content of the bubbles on your diagram will depend on your product idea. Your diagram may look somewhat different, but the concept does not change. This diagram will help you identify the sliver that needs you the most *now*. These are the people who have a problem and are willing and able to spend money to solve that problem.

Let's look at another example: In the diagram above, one bubble may represent Spanish-speaking students. Perhaps your research shows that you can find tutors who are willing to teach Spanish and that students are more eager to pay for help in that subject area. As a result, your focus may change to that market segment for initial deployment of your tutoring service.

Having this degree of clarity is priceless! You must talk to enough students and teachers and ask the right questions (see Section 2) in order to get this clarity. You must do all of this before you start your business.

Chapter 11

Estimating Market Size

ONE OF THE MOST important things for entrepreneurs to remember is to pick large markets. Sizing your target market is very important, and large markets attract more investors as they provide more opportunities for companies to grow. Large markets are also more tolerant of the missteps that you are likely to make. Actually, from the point of view of an investor or VC, market dynamics and size is the most important of the three criteria to take into consideration when deciding to invest (the others being team caliber and the uniqueness of the solution provided by the company, in that order).

There is nothing wrong with small markets. It's just that if your market is too small, it will be harder for you to make money or attract investors. You will also have less room for errors and will need to be accurate in most of your decisions in order to accomplish your goals.

A large and growing market, however, can be very forgiving. You can mess up on half of your actions and decisions and still get a piece of a large market. Large and growing markets attract bigger players and a lot more competition, but this, too, can work in your favor. A large market will create the awareness and consumer demand for your product or service, and you will be able to serve this market with a solution that is better, more customized, or simply, unique.

Small Markets

Small markets are, by nature, concentrated and, thus, very often protected by high entry barriers. This means that the number of people that needs the solution provided by the market is small or that some company has strong patents and other restrictions that limit the ability for competitors to enter the market. This also means that you may have difficulty entering this segment of the market. If, even after all your hard work, you do not have enough customers to sell your product to, it would be a real shame.

Small Segments of Large Markets are Attractive

For large, billion-dollar-revenue companies, the market segments have to be very large. HP and Cisco, for example, will not bother to get involved in a market segment unless it will bring in at least $100 million in annual revenue. Anything smaller does not make the needle move on their performance meter. But small markets can prove to be big enough to allow a small, innovative startup company to get a foothold.

11.1 Small Markets are OK

Market size matters. You want to go after the biggest opportunity available (starting, of course, with a sliver of the big market initially, so you can get a foothold). There is nothing wrong with small markets, however. Small markets may be attractive because they will probably provide less competition. If you have some unique specialty or expertise that allows you to service a small market, you are less likely to have a competitor coming in and stealing your customers. A unique idea in a small market can lead to a good living. Just to clarify, when I say "small market," I'm talking about a 10 to 20 million dollar market.

Venture capitalists (VCs) and other investors have bigger numbers in mind. They consider $100 million to be a small market. Half-a-billion to a billion dollars is a medium market. They want to invest in markets that are or can rapidly grow to be over a billion dollars a year. Only then do their investments have a chance to grow and become significant enough to matter and allow them to make the returns that they want to make. (For more on this, see my other book "Get Funded!" at www.FiveMountainPress.com.)

> **Small Markets**
> **(continued)**
>
> Due to these restrictions of entry, a unique idea based in a small market industry could lead to great success, but it may have trouble getting investors, especially VCs, interested in providing funding. These investors want to go after large and fast-growing markets. They know that even if you miss the mark and do not deliver exactly the product that you promised or are simply late in delivering your product, you may still get enough revenue in a large, growing market.

11.2 Large Markets Offer Bigger Sandboxes

Most venture capitalists look at multibillion dollar markets. This is because precision is necessary to fit into a small market. If you are trying to do so, it's like trying to hit a dartboard from across the room. You have to be very good, very accurate, and very lucky to be able to hit the board, let alone the bull's eye. All of your business decisions have to be correct.

But, if you are trying to address a growing or large market, it's like hitting the wall from the opposite side of the room. It's much easier to do. Even if half of your decisions are wrong, you may still hit part of your target market.

11.3 Growing Markets

With growing markets, the players and the status quo are always changing. A startup company can attack the underbelly of the beast, creating a foothold for itself. This is the art of spotting a crack in the armor of the big players, identifying a niche or a subsegment that is not being well served and coming in and carving a niche of your own. We see this occurring throughout history. While big beverage companies were making drinks for the world population, a small company in California determined that there was an unmet need for healthy and organic real fruit juices. It realized that people are willing to pay three to four times more money than they used to pay for drinks in order to get healthy juices that were tasty and natural. It is for this reason Odwalla Juice Company was formed and ended up becoming a big success story.

Since it takes a new company a few years to grow up (i.e., to become established with predictable revenue streams and to have solid customers), it is perfectly OK to look for markets that may be small right now but could become very big by the time you are ready to actually sell your product.

An example of this sort of growth can be found in the infrastructure for the next generation of wireless communications. As 3G infrastructure (the third generation of wireless technology that provides megabit per second upload and download speeds for your mobile phones) is currently being deployed, more and more companies are making a big deal about using 3G networks. There is plenty of evidence, however, that in three to four years there will be a need for a fourth generation of wireless infrastructure, or 4G networks. Companies starting up now will not see this 4G communication infrastructure market, even if they look for it, but three to four years from now, it is expected to be worth tens of billions of dollars.

> **Shoot Where the Duck Will Be**
>
> "You need to shoot where the duck will be, not where the duck is," is commonly heard advice among duck hunters. Entrepreneurs, too, must learn to predict the location of their proverbial duck and must be able to estimate where the market will be when they are ready to engage.

11.4 TAM and the Market Size

You may have heard the acronym TAM (total available market) and references to the concept of a market size, and you may be wondering exactly what these terms mean and which one is relevant to you. TAM is the number of **potential** purchases of your product or service in one year multiplied by the price of your product or service. If everybody in the world—or the United States, depending on what your target market is—could potentially buy one of the products or services you are selling in one year, then you would multiply the total population by the price of each sale

TAM vs. Market Size

TAM (Total Available Market): the amount of revenue your company would derive from the market if everyone were to buy your product. This is how you can express the total market size for a new or emerging market. For established markets, however, the market size is usually determined by the actual annual revenue of all companies that are selling in that market. For example, the U.S. automobile market would be the combined revenue of all auto companies that sell in the U.S. market. This is how you would express the market size for cars in the U.S. But, for the electric car market (which does not yet exist), you may talk about it as if all cars were electric and then the market size would be the annual number of cars sold in the U.S. multiplied by the average price of an electric car.

to determine your total available market. Market size is usually expressed in terms of dollars (or units of currency).

What is the TAM for Coca Cola in the U.S.? Of course, Coca Cola sells worldwide, but for the sake of example, let's look at the TAM for Coke in the U.S. alone. Let's also say that only people between the ages of 6 and 80 drink Coke products. So, how many people are there in the U.S., from age 6 to age 80, and how much will the average person drink per year? For example, if you assume people average one beverage per day, you would take 365 beverages per year, multiply it by the total U.S. population between the ages of 6 and 80, and multiply that number by the cost of the beverage. You would now have calculated your TAM. If every American between the ages of 6 and 80 bought Coke products, this is how much revenue Coke would derive from the U.S. market.

What is My Market Size?

Now you know how to compute the total available market, or TAM. As a startup, you know you're not going to be able to provide a product or service to every person in the United States, but you can determine what the size of your market will be once you have fully grown and developed your company.

The "market size," as commonly used by entrepreneurs and investors for established markets, is the actual market served. It is the total revenue of all companies that are trying to sell into this market. This number approaches TAM for established markets, such as the Coca Cola market or the market for headache medicines. Since you are a startup, you will serve a smaller portion of this market initially. You will start with a small beachhead—the piece of the market that you are trying to conquer first, the sliver!

Markets develop and get larger and smaller every year based on the actual sales and the ability of customers to spend money. But for emerging markets for new products and technologies, there is no such thing as the total revenue of all companies. It is not an established market. In this case, how does an entrepreneur go about estimating the market size? For this, I suggest using the following formula:

Total Market size = **the number of all the people who can buy the product**

X **the number of times they buy per year**

X **the price of my product**

Example #1:

There are 300 million people in the United States, and the total number of households is approximately 100 million. If every home can buy one electronic water purifier system priced around $500, and they each buy a new system every 10 years, then the TAM in the U.S. is 100 million x 0.10 x $500 = $5 billion.

Example #2:

Say you run an Indian restaurant in a town with a population of 100,000. In this town, 70,000 people are in the age group that is likely to eat at a restaurant of any kind. Based on surveys and research, you find that only 10% of the people who eat at restaurants are actually likely to buy Indian food. This brings the target segment of the population–meaning, the number of people that you plan to lure to eat at your restaurant–to approximately 7,000 people. If, on average, a meal costs $20 per person, then $20 x 7,000, or $140,000, is the potential revenue from these customers. If it can be established that these people are likely to eat out at an Indian restaurant once a month (i.e., 12 times a year), then the market size for this town will be 12 x $140,000, or $1.68 million per year. In reality, however, you will never get the whole market; you will only get a portion of this market since others will be competing with you to get a piece of this pie. Besides, there is no way you could actually service everyone in the town. Nevertheless, total market size defines the upper bounds to this market. From here, you can see the actual served part of this market and how you may participate in your new venture and expand your market.

If you're only able to serve 2,000 customers during the first year your restaurant is in business, your market size doesn't change for the next year. Market size is determined by potential, so it remains at 1.68 million. Think of it this way: your market size consists of every individual who is capable of purchasing your product or service and who you are able to convince to become a customer.

Example #3:

Pretend you are making some kind of instrument for left-handed dentists. You will need to figure out the total number of left-handed dentists in the country. In order to do this, you must first figure out the total number of dentists in the country. (A quick visit to www.ada.org, the American Dental Association website, reveals that there are 155,000 dentists in the U.S.) Then, you must calculate the percentage of the general population that is left-handed. (The Census Bureau website, www.census.gov, and the website for the trade association that serves dentists would be great places to find this type of data.) Multiply that percentage by the total number of dentists, and you have the approximate number of left-handed dentists in the country.

Revenue vs. Market Size

Your revenue potential is not your market size. Market size is determined by potential to sell to all likely target customers. It reflects the total revenue potential only if everyone who could realistically buy does buy. Your revenue potential will be a small subset of this market size number. It is the expected revenue based on your ability to sell to a sliver of the total potential market. It takes a long time before a company can grow to reach all of its potential customers. Remember, it took Coca Cola over 100 years to reach most of its potential customers. Your revenue will a very small fraction of your potential market size.

Section 3

If there is approximately one dentist per 2,000 people and there are more than 300 million people in the United States, then there are approximately 150,000 dentists in the country. If 10% of all dentists are left-handed, you would have a market of 15,000 left-handed dentists. If you're selling your dental instrument at a retail cost of $1,000 and every left-handed dentist buys one each year, then your total market size is 15,000 x $1000, or $15 million per year, which may be large enough for you to have a small business but, perhaps, not large enough to attract professional investors into your company. Your projected revenue will be a fraction of this $15 million since you are unlikely to get to all of the customers.

Of course, when you start selling, you may only be selling to the dentists where you live, or you may go through a distribution company that only sells to dentists in the western United States. If, for example, you initially can only focus on Los Angeles and San Francisco, you may only target 500 dentists, or maybe just 200 dentists. Then, your initial revenue projections will only be based on 200 to 500 dentists; but your annual total available market (TAM) will still be computed for 15,000 dentists times the cost of the instrument.

11.5 What is Bottom-Up Analysis?

Up to this point, I have been showing top-down analyses. A top-down analysis starts with the total population—figuring out the total number of dentists, for example, and then calculating the number of left-handed dentists. But a bottom-up analysis is calculated in the opposite way: by adding everybody who really would buy your product or service, one by one. For example, if you are planning to sell a product that can potentially be bought by any college student, then your TAM is computed by the total number of all college students in the target region.

But if you plan to sell on the campus of the town that you live in, the population of that campus will determine the bottom-up calculation for your startup.

> **Top-Down Analysis:**
> Start with the total market and then work down to look at the market segment.
>
> **Bottom-Up Analysis:**
> Look at the product and then determine the number of users.

An excellent source for bottom-up analyses is the U.S. Census Bureau. This data is free and can be very helpful in determining the number of people in any segment in the United States as it provides all sorts of data according to gender, geography, occupation, and age. The website, www.census.gov, is full of useful information.

Section 3

There is a wealth of information on this website that can help you size your market. Through these valuable reports, you can extract the metrics that can help you size your target market.

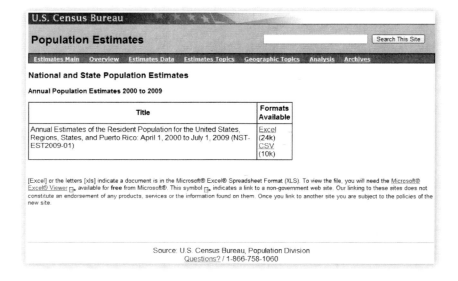

Initially, you may only be considering how many dentists you can reach in the city or state you live in, and who you can reach may also depend on your distribution partners. Distribution partners are the companies through whom you will sell your product. Unless you plan to sell on the Internet directly to dentists, it is important to understand through your market research how your customers typically buy such products. The local distributors are your channel to the consumers. You don't have to go through them, but it is not easy to change the buying habits of the consumers.

11.6 Where Can I Find Top-Down Numbers?

Top-down numbers can be found by searching within the market research reports or prospectuses of companies that have gone public. Research reports on these companies may be available on the Internet or at your local library. (These sources are discussed in more detail in Chapter 9.)

11.7 How Do I Use Top-Down Numbers?

When developing an idea, entrepreneurs (and their investors) want to know how big is the business opportunity; will it make enough money if the idea is developed and sold; are there enough people willing to spend the money to create decent revenue for your company; and, most of all, is it worth your time? You need to have these questions answered before you start your startup. The reason you are doing all of this analysis and research is, in fact, to find out if your business venture is worth your time and if you should even go down this path. In truth, there is no sense in starting down this path if the total number of potential customers is extremely small. If you somehow don't meet consumers' needs or you don't connect with them, all of your effort will be wasted because there is not enough of a market for your product or service.

This is where the top-down market analysis is useful. The number that results from a top-down analysis defines your maximum potential opportunity. In the example discussed earlier of the Indian restaurant, it is established that the maximum yearly potential for Indian restaurants is $1.68M annually–to be split between all businesses who can serve the target population. Unless you expand or do other innovative things to change consumer behavior, that will be the ceiling of revenue for your Indian restaurant venture.

It is for this reason that many web-based businesses are very attractive. Because they are highly scalable, the number of people they can reach is almost unlimited. For example, if, instead of making a device for left-handed dentists, you created a web portal of valuable information that could be used by all dentists, then your potential U.S. market would be much bigger. You might even find an international audience. The important thing is that, no matter what your product or service is, you need to make sure there are enough people in your target market who will be interested in what you have to offer.

In conclusion, once you are done with your market research, you should be able to draw a picture like the one below. This picture shows the overall market and how it grows each year. It also indicates that your portion of the target segment (in blue) is growing. In this hypothetical picture, the colors may indicate various portions or segments of the target market. For example, this chart may represent the number of mobile handsets sold, with blue indicating smart phones (with Internet access) and red indicating the number of phones with built-in video cameras. Since your product only works with smart phones, the color blue indicates your market growth; but one can see the overall market-size growth and how a product line may be developed to gain additional market share.

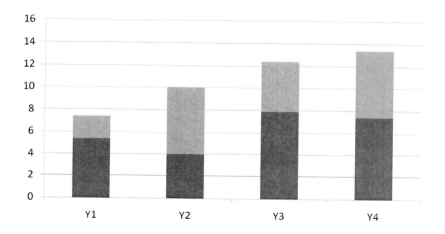

Chapter 12

Identifying a Business Model

A BUSINESS MODEL is simply the description of how a business makes money. It involves the issues of who pays whom and how much is left in the business owner's pocket at the end of the day. In this chapter, I will help you develop and better understand your business model, which will show how your business will make money, how much money it will make, and through what sales channel that money will be made. One of the key concepts in your business model definition is how much you will make per transaction—what comes in and what leaves on a per transaction basis.

You may invest thousands, even millions, of dollars in developing a product or service. It will cost you a certain fixed amount to run the operations on a monthly basis, e.g., salaries and rent, and there are variable costs for each recurring transaction. In your business model, you clearly show how much you are making on a **per transaction basis**. On each product that you sell, how

Gross Profit

Gross Profit is the amount of money left after you subtract costs of sales from your total revenue. Cost of Sales includes the cost of goods that you are selling and any direct selling costs associated with those sales; for example, if you sell a widget on the Internet for $9, you buy this widget for $2, and it also costs you $1 for freight and warehousing and $3 for advertizing on the Internet, then your gross profit is $9 - $2-$1-$3 = $4 per widget. Now you will have to pay for employees, salaries, rent, and other R&D (research and development) expenses from this gross profit. But if this gross profit is not a healthy number, you will not have enough to pay for these fixed expenses.

much will you make? This is the "gross profit." If this number is healthy, you will have plenty of money for fixed costs and still have some money left in your pocket, i.e., your net income. (For more on these topics related to finance, please read my other book, *Finance Essentials for Entrepreneurs*. It is available from www.FiveMountainPess.com.)

In order to figure out your business model (how your business will make money, from whom and how much), you must first understand who are the "characters" in the "play" that you are directing (i.e., your startup) and how they interact. You may have customers, vendors, affiliates, and other characters. Once you can list them all on a page, you can see who pays whom and how money travels from one person to another. This is the clarity that a business model provides. It helps you see what your sources of revenue and what your sources of variable expenses are. It helps you understand how you make money.

For your business model, you should be able to draw some version of the picture below:

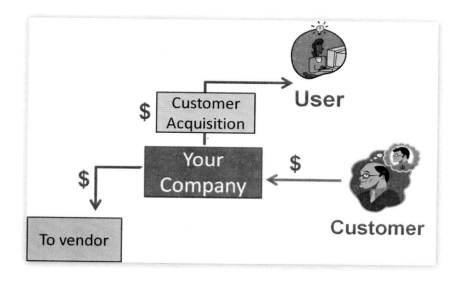

This picture gives some idea as to how much money you'll make on each transaction. Developing this understanding now is part of the essential market research that I want you to do before you start your business. It will save you a lot of time and heartache later. This information will become clear as you do the research as defined in Section 2 of this book. You will study how your competitors make money and how you can do the same. You will see who really pays you and who else do you have to pay.

Note that the picture above may not seem complete to you. It is not supposed to be. This is not a full diagram of the finances for your startup. It just deals with the business model. You don't need to worry about all of the fixed costs that got you to the point of being able to sell your product. You will deal with those details when you build the financial model. The financial model with include startup costs and fixed costs such as your rent, salaries, and overhead. The purpose of this picture is to help you understand how much gross profit you will earn on each transaction and, if you do, where does will it come from.

Unit Economics

You should be clear about how your business will make money; for this purpose, unit economics is a key concept to understand. The "unit" in unit economics can be a single product or one service transaction, or it can be one city, one school, or one restaurant. It depends on your business. What the right unit is will depend on your own business understanding. The key point here is that you must define a unit and make sure that you know the revenue and the costs associated with serving that one unit. You should also make sure that each unit generates enough profit.

Computing Product Cost

Next, if you are dealing with physical products (versus services), you should compute your cost of manufacturing for each subsequent item. In other words, do not include the cost of making the very first product, as that is always much more expensive due to the set-up costs involved. Add in the cost of selling each one, including charges such as shipping, packaging, and freight costs. You should also include any licensing fees that are placed on each unit shipped. And don't forget to compute your customer acquisition costs. These can be discounts and incentives you give to your channel partners (i.e., your sales channel, or the people who actually buy from you and sell your products in a store); affiliate fees that you pay; or the amount you spend, per customer, on Google or Facebook ads—if you plan to acquire customers this way. Add these numbers up and see how much is left in your pocket before you subtract the fixed costs.

There has to be sufficient profit in each transaction for the company to have a chance to pay for its fixed costs and be able to scale the business. For example, if you sold a widget for $9 (the example we considered earlier), your customer acquisition cost was $4, and your manufacturing and shipping costs added up to $1, then your gross profit is $9-$3-$1, or $5. If you sell one million widgets per year, then your annual gross profit will be $5 million. If your company fixed costs are $3 million a year, then you can estimate a net income (before taxes and depreciation) of $5 million-$3 million, or $2 million.

The main issue here is that you must ensure that your gross profits are healthy. If there is not enough gross profit, you will not be able to run a business that generates sufficient cash or is interesting to investors.

Do your business economics work out this way? What are your main financial assumptions? How will you track these numbers and make sure that there is not a huge deviation from them? If your business relies on making widgets for $9 and your customer acquisition cost is $3, then you will need to keep a close eye on these

New Business Model

Inventing a new business model is not the smartest thing for an entrepreneur to do. Old habits are hard to change. Yes, iTunes brought a new business model to the way songs can be purchased, and Geico did the same for auto insurance when it created a way for it to be purchased online; but these companies had a great deal of marketing strength that they used to convince people to adopt these new business models. Most entrepreneurs are not that powerful. Try to find a business model that already works for someone else; innovate in other ways. It is hard to change the ways people are used to buying a certain product or service.

numbers. If you measure these numbers and see them deviate, then you must take corrective measures. Unfortunately, most entrepreneurs do not even know what their key financial metrics are and do not track or measure them. When their businesses decline, they blame factors such the economy, labor issues, or some other random phenomena.

You need to be clear about your business model before you are done with your market research. Ask people questions and study surveys to help figure out how money will be made on each of your business transactions. Study the filings—such as the SEC filings—from other companies in your industry to see how those companies make money. Discover what channels they use and what their key metrics and KPIs (key performance indicators) are. Compare your key financial assumptions (about cost, price, customer acquisition costs, and manufacturing costs) and KPIs to theirs to ensure that you are within a reasonable range of your competitors and that you are able to explain them.

For example, if your sales and marketing costs are 15% of your revenue after a few years of steady operations, but your competitors are all within a range of 28% to 34%, then you'd better be able to explain why your numbers are so different. If you are somewhere between 24% and 38%, then you are within the ballpark. Study the competition to learn their metrics, price points, and channel choices; and make sure you can explain or justify any deviation you may have from them. Your investors will be asking you these kinds of questions.

The questions you asked for your market research will help you draw up your business model. Although the business model is something that most entrepreneurs do not spend much time putting together, this is a big mistake.

Let me give you one example: I was once working with a startup company (called Ad Insight) that did sentiment analysis on the web for companies launching new products. Their software used Syntax and other complicated language processing to scour the web and look at blogs and discussion forums to decide if the reviews of new products were favorable or not. It took us a while to realize that while our customers were generally advertising firms doing product launches, the sentiment data actually came from users. Drawing the following picture made it easier to create a business model that helped us understand the unit economics involved.

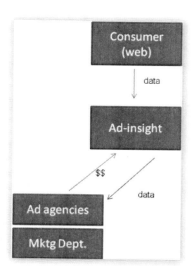

Section 3

The bottom line is your market research should help you clarify the following issues:

1) Who do you sell to, and who else is involved in making this sale happen?

2) How much does each party get paid, and how does the money travel from the customer's pocket to your pocket? (Also, how much is left within the company to pay for fixed expenses and how much is left at the end of the year as profit?)

The ability to answer these questions will force you to think hard about the viability and potential prosperity of your startup and ask the right questions. It will also force you to think about what to watch out for regarding your KPI and to create a dashboard (a set of indicators that tell you about the health of your company) to watch over your business as it grows.

Chapter 13

Creating Market Positioning

Identifying the Competition

Before you begin your business, one of the most important things for you to consider is how your customers and users will view your product or service when it is compared to the other options available. This is called positioning. Your positioning is nothing more than what real estate you occupy in the minds of your users and customers—how they see you. You reinforce your positioning by stating it, providing proof that you really are able to claim it, and continuously reinforcing it over a long period of time.

Positioning is not always based on fact

For example, most people would agree that the safest car you can drive in America is a Volvo. Volvo has worked very hard to occupy that market positioning in people's minds. The fact is, however, if you look at the real crash-test data, Volvo is not even in one of the top three spots; instead, it usually places in the sixth, seventh, or eighth spot. But by using its boxy design to reinforce those messages of safety, Volvo has been able to occupy a premium position when it comes to safety in people's minds.

Similarly, when you think of Walmart, you think of low prices, because that is the market positioning this store has reinforced time after time, through commercial after commercial. It is considered the low-cost retailer.

How do you know that you are done with the market research necessary for positioning your company? If you are able to draw a picture similar to the one below, then you are done with the initial phase of positioning. This requires you to know the market, its players, and your differentiation well.

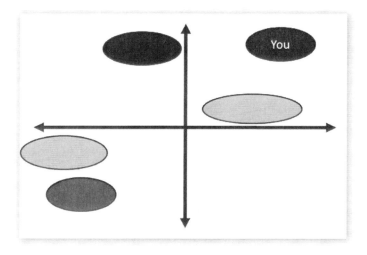

Ask yourself the following questions: For your own business, what position do you need to occupy? Is your product the easiest to use? Is your product or service the most technologically advanced? Are you the best looking company? Is your product the most comfortable to apply?

You must profoundly study and understand your competitors in order to find a positioning that makes your product or service look different—and better—than your competitors in some aspects. You must realize, however, that you are not going to look better than your competition across the board, especially if you are just starting a business, so what you are looking for are differences that customers will appreciate and desire. Once you create those differences, you can get a foothold in the customer mindset, and, then, you can start your business.

For example, let's say you are starting a coffee shop. Of course, there are already other coffee shops in the same neighborhood, but, in addition to coffee, you also have French pastries to serve in your coffee shop. Although not everyone is going to like French pastries, some people like French pastries with their coffee, and they will be attracted to your shop. Alternatively, you may offer more comfortable seating than the other shops. Instead of chairs, you can have sofas. Or maybe you play a certain kind of music in the background. Somehow, you differentiate yourself from the other coffee shops in the neighborhood, thus attracting a certain clientele.

> **Know everything about your competitors!**
>
> Small, unnoticeable differences between you and your competitors will not convince consumers to buy your product or service over a competitor's. Be sure to research details about your competitors, and then add new features to your product or service that will make it more noticeable and attractive to consumers. Smart phones, for example, have trumped basic phones in recent years due to their Internet-everywhere feature. Find a feature that distinguishes your product or service from your competitors'. If you can't, go back to the drawing board.

Another good example would be a high-tech or nonconsumer business dealing with social networking. Like your competition, you offer photo sharing, for example, but unlike the other companies, you also share music and videos. With the music and video sharing, you have differentiated your positioning.

It is vital that you study the market, understand who the players are, figure out how you can be different, and know the people who will care about that difference. At that point, you have established your market.

Until you figure out your niche market (the very first segment or part of the target market that you will address first), it will be hard for you to pinpoint your competition. You might think your competition consists of Companies A, B, and C, but, with the way you are being positioned in the customer's mind, your clientele may think your competition is Company X, Y, or Z. So, it is important to not only identify your competition but also validate that assumption by talking to users and customers in informal conversations, in group settings, or through surveys.

13.1 What Segment of the Market to Address First?

Your research about what market segment you plan to address first will help you understand its landscape. This includes understanding who else is likely to be in your customers' view when they look for the solution that you are trying to provide. You must learn to see the world from the customer's point of view. This is why I insist that you ask leading questions and then listen to your potential customers during your interviews. Do not start telling them about your great new "invention."

Suppose, once again, that you have an answer for dentists who want to build their businesses. Perhaps your solution is a better fit for certain segments of the market. Maybe it's Asian dentists because you have connections with Asian communities, and you are able to market to them because you understand where they live and congregate. Since you have a unique advantage over competitors who may be marketing to these dentists, this is the segment of the market you will attempt to make your own.

13.2 Coming Up with Your Company's Positioning

Once you understand your segment of the market, you will be better able to recognize your competition and to come up with the positioning statement that will make you appear better than them. Are you the most expensive option, the coolest, the one in multiple colors, or the most advanced technologically? Pick one and do not try to mix many of these attributes as that will make you appear confusing and, hence, forgettable in your customer's mind. The temptation will be to think your product is applicable to several segments of the market. While it's understandable

"Cheapest" is not a good positioning statement (in most cases)

My least favorite market positioning is "cheapest"; it is not a good positioning for a startup. All your competition has to do to drive you out of business is lower its prices temporarily. It would only work if, due to some technological or operational innovation, you're able to change the way your product is delivered and, hence, develop a long-term sustainable cost advantage over your competitors.

that you don't want to limit yourself to just one segment and you may have trouble deciding which segment is most compelling, don't make the mistake of trying to do too much.

Position Yourself

You want to position yourself in the minds of your customers. It is though positioning that you make them think about your company in the way that you want them to. It creates a certain image about your product or service that could prove to be beneficial or, if done incorrectly, detrimental to your company. For example, when you think of cars, which car is considered the safest? Many people would say Volvo. That is the position that Volvo has been able to create for itself through years of persistent advertising. Even though the facts don't actually support this claim, the positioning is etched in people's minds. This concept also applies to your company, and even yourself.

As a startup company, you have very limited resources. So, you have to understand where to focus your efforts. If you have only a few arrows in your quiver, each arrow counts and you can't afford to misfire. That's why it's so important to take the time to identify your market segment and to study who is serving that segment. You need to figure out your competition's weakness–the underbelly of the beast. Only then will you be able to go to through the process of discovering your own strengths, creating a positioning that exploits your competitors' weaknesses, and determining whether customers are looking for an alternate solution. This will give you the best chance to succeed.

Somehow, when it comes to business, people get away from looking at competitive positioning in a rigorous manner—the way it should be done.

A Personal Story: Positioning Yourself for Success

When I was in high school, I really wanted to be on the field hockey team even though I wasn't really that good at field hockey. In order to make the team, I had to compete against others and work very hard.

At that time, I did a similar analysis of my competition (though not as rigorous as the ones I do for business today) in order to position myself against them (in this case, the other players who were eager to make the varsity team). I talked to different people on the field hockey team to learn about the team's weakest spot. I discovered that the goalie position had no backup. In addition to that, the one guy who played goalie was only half-heartedly into the game. Every other position on the team had a lot of competition. So, guess what I did. I applied to be goalie. Since I was the only person who wanted that position, I only had to be slightly better than the one guy who held that position already. Voila! Three months later, I was wearing the team colors. I had made the high school collegiate field hockey team as goalie.

I do not recommend that you position yourself as the lowest-priced product or service. To be the lowest priced, you must either compromise quality or have an extremely heavy investment in technology and the supply chain. Companies like Walmart have spent billions of dollars to achieve that positioning; it's not easy to do. For a startup company, being a low-cost leader is usually not ideal. You can easily be beaten as your competition simply lowers its prices and edges you out of the market.

13.3 Validating Your Positioning Assumptions

Whatever positioning you come up with, you must be sure to validate the assumptions that brought you there. There's nothing worse than your company being in the wrong position. Do not fall into the trap of thinking that your business is good for one reason while your customers are buying your product or service for completely different reasons. You need to carefully monitor your position. Talk to your customers, and do surveys to validate your assumptions. Imagine your situation if you thought your customers were buying your product because it was technologically advanced and easy to use. Your advertising dollars, communication presentations, and conversations with clients would emphasize those particular strengths. Your assumptions would prove to be incorrect, however, if your customers actually used your product because of an additional feature, or two, that your competitors' products lacked. Your product might have been neither easier nor cheaper than the competitors' products, but it was able to integrate with Microsoft Outlook, a benefit that customers needed.

Sometimes Positioning Should Be Tested and Modified

Do not make the mistake of simply assuming that your positioning is correct. You have to validate your positioning because you are spending a lot of time, energy, and money in your efforts to reinforce it. Are customers buying your assertion? Does it make sense to people based on the facts you provide? For example, if you make the positioning statement that you have the most hygienic food preparation and the cleanest restaurant in the business but your dirty restrooms are not reflective of that position, it will be hard to make this positioning stick in the consumer's mind. Likewise, it will be hard to assert that your company has the most technologically advanced adaptive antenna technology when there is simply no one on your team who has the credentials to make this believable.

13.4 What if There Is No Competition?

If entrepreneurs believe there is no competition for their product or service, it usually means they have not done their homework and have incorrectly identified either the market segment they should be focusing on or the other players in their segment. Occasionally, there might actually be no competition, but this is extremely rare, occurring only when a product or service is new and innovative. Even then, the idea that one has no competition should be viewed with skepticism. The competition is probably out there. It just needs to be found.

> **There is just about always competition!**
>
> Any entrepreneur who believes there is no competition for his or her product or service has not done sufficient market research. Though there might not be direct competition, there will always be some sort of indirect competition, such as a seemingly different product or a service that does a slightly similar task.

The human race has survived for 10 to 15 thousand years and even put a man on the moon without having many of the things that you may be inventing or trying to do today. **The fact that there is no competition may indicate that there is no need.**

> **There is just about always competition!** (continued)
>
> Sometimes, even if there is no obvious competition from other companies, the mere fact that customers must find some way of addressing a problem that is a pressing need serves as the competition in itself. In other words, doing nothing (or the status quo) is your competition. For example, when microwave ovens were coming on the market, there was no particular competition other than status quo. We could simply let the meals cook at the speed we had always cooked them. Doing nothing was the competition.

Try to talk to dozens of your potential buyers and customers, and ask what you can do today to answer their unmet needs. Find out what alternatives they have considered, and discuss why no purchase was made or why an alternative didn't work out. Finally, ask what they would like to see in a new product or service in this particular area. If asked correctly, these questions should result in answers that reveal a lot. You should learn if there is really a need, how big the need is, and how much people are willing to invest in the solution.

Before you even start your business, you need to ask the questions to learn this information and more, without revealing how you may be trying to solve the problem at hand. You need to really understand what the customer wants if you are to succeed in your endeavor. So, do your homework, find your market niche, and concentrate on how to become the best of the best.

Section 4

What Is Next?

Once you have done your market research well enough to get clarity on your target segment, positioning, business model, and market sizing, congratulate yourself! You are already in the top 5% of all entrepreneurs. Most people jump right into their ventures without ever finishing this homework. I should know; I used to be one of them.

Now, it is time to start moving forward again and start writing down what you have learned. You will be constantly validating your assumptions during this stage of your market research. You will change your mind and your business plan several times over the next few months—and that is a good thing. All ideas have to be chiseled away at to become good. This is normal and should be welcomed. You should be flexible in your execution while remaining true to your vision and motivations.

Let's look at what else you should be doing to maintain your forward momentum. As you start developing a business plan, be sure to write down your findings. The best companies collect a lot of data from customer interactions and secondary market research, and they let that data drive their vision and execution.

Chapter 14

Developing Your Own Metrics and Validating Your Assumptions

EACH BUSINESS RUNS on certain key assumptions. These assumptions can range anywhere from how much you can charge for your product to how much will it cost to produce it to how many people may buy it. They are made during the market research phase of development. You must learn which three, four, or five key assumptions underlie your business model, and then you should constantly test them for correctness and accuracy. Let's take a closer look at this concept.

14.1 Key Assumptions

Three or four assumptions drive the basic economics of every business or product. After talking to customers, you can identify those main assumptions on which your business will run. Then, you need to make sure you have a way to test your assumptions and see if they are really true. Continue to conduct tests from time to time to validate your assumptions and tweak them as needed.

14.2 Identifying Your Assumptions and Metrics

You must be able to list the certain assumptions that are key to your business's success. If you are making widgets, for example, the assumptions may deal with the cost of making these widgets, the cost of freight, and the cost of commissions you may pay to have them sold. You should study your particular startup and establish what you should measure. Once you have identified these three to five main assumptions, then you need to come up with a suitable value for each of them. Only then can a simple financial analysis reveal the viability of your business.

Suppose you're starting a restaurant and your assumptions are based on how much each table earns on average. These include your make assumptions about the number of times you turn over the tables and seat new customers each night, your daily occupancy rate, and the number of tables filled. These three assumptions are very critical, and they can drive a lot of the economics and purchasing decisions you make. Let us examine what the key assumptions are and how does one establish these Key Performance Indicators (KPIs) that drive your business.

14.3 Testing Your Assumptions

Once you have certain assumptions, you need to ask yourself what is a reasonable value for each of them. You can do this through market research. In the restaurant example above, you would want to hang out in restaurants already in the neighborhood where you are planning to open your own. For several days, you should observe how often they turn their tables per night and how long people typically sit at a table. You might befriend some of the waiters and try to get an informal idea as to how much people are spending per table. You can even talk to some customers, if appropriate. Or you can stand outside the window from time to time and gauge a restaurant's occupancy rate, i.e., the number of tables filled at any given time. This is how one tests one's assumptions. It is an ongoing process, and you may repeat it every month or every few weeks.

> **Assumptions and Metrics**
>
> Assumptions are another form of market research that can benefit your company greatly. In order to correctly gauge the opportunity that your business carries, a smart entrepreneur makes assumptions about certain aspects of the business. Estimating the average expenditure on your product or monitoring consumer trends in a prominent neighborhood, for example, can both lead to useful assumptions for your business. These become the metrics on how you will judge the success of your venture.

14.4 Using Your Assumptions for Financial Modeling

These assumptions are also key to building a simple financial model, perhaps an income statement, when you are trying to convince yourself that this venture will make sufficient profit to be an interesting and sustainable business. If your main assumptions regarding restaurants like the one you plan to open are that each table turns over with new guests three times a night, guests spend $42 on average, and there is a 70% occupancy rate, then you can build a profit and loss model based on that data. You can figure out how many people you'll need to hire and what kind of food you'll serve. If any one of your assumptions changes, it will have a significant impact on your business.

14.5 Revisit and Tweak

Once you start your business, you will need a test to see what is actually happening with your product or service. In your restaurant, for example, if you are turning tables only two times a night, then you might need to remedy the situation by changing the music in the restaurant to a faster tempo. Or you may need to hire speedier waiters who can be more efficient in turning the tables. If people are spending less than the $42 that you assumed they would be spending on average, then you will need to make other changes. You might consider different menu items, perhaps adding some new appetizers or a more extensive wine or dessert list, to make people spend a little bit more money so you can meet your assumption. If you don't know what your main assumptions are, you don't know what to tweak.

No matter what, your business must have main assumptions. For another example, let's say you are assuming you will use Google ads and a landing page to increase the customer traffic for your business. If you do, then you will need to monitor your click rate and your click through rate. How many people get to your landing page because they click on your Google ad while they're surfing the web? How many people who visit your landing page actually click to take further action? If these numbers are below your target range, then you will need to change the landing page copy, change the wording in your Google ads, or maybe hire an expert to help you. But if you don't know what numbers you're looking for and you're not paying attention to them, it's easy to not think about them for several months. If that's the case, then you are not operating your business efficiently. Knowing your three or four key metrics is very important in running your business.

These assumptions then become the metrics on how you may judge the performance of your business. They become the dashboard of your venture. You should learn to revisit these assumptions once a year to make sure that they still make sense, but you should also be watching your numbers several times a month to keep your eye on the ball.

Chapter 15

Next Steps for Your Venture

CONGRATULATE YOURSELF AGAIN for getting this far (unless, of course, you have jumped ahead to read the end of this book). I hope you did learn a few ideas on how to conduct market research on a shoestring budget. It is time consuming and difficult, but it is essential to your company's future viability and well-being. All great entrepreneurs do some kind of market research and validation of their initial assumptions.

Now it is time to start assembling a team and thinking about other aspects of your business, including:

1) Legal incorporation
2) Funding strategy (How much do you need and when?)
3) Go-to market strategy (How will you get your first 10 customers?)
4) Financial model (How much money will you make, and what key assumptions do you base that amount on?)

5) Hiring a team that will help you achieve your goals

6) Product development and testing

Once you have these aspects figured out, you will be in a position to integrate them with the four main questions that you answered in this book:

1) Is there a true unmet need and who has this need? (Market research and segmentation)

2) Who is trying to serve this need and why is it unmet? (Positioning)

3) How big is this opportunity and is it worth my time? (Market sizing)

4) How will I make money and how much money can this business make? (Business model)

The 14 sections in this book instruct you in writing your business plan. An executive summary and an investor presentation will soon be needed. These sections represent the paragraphs in an executive summary as well as the ten PowerPoint slides in your 20-minute investor pitch. Remember that all generals need commanders. Who will be on your team? You must start thinking about recruiting early employees, cofounders, and advisory board members who will help you get started. (I have more on this in my book about teams.)

Starting your own business is a rewarding, yet difficult, journey. I look forward to keeping you company as you begin your own business. Let's stay in touch!

Epilogue

I HOPE THIS BOOK serves as a useful checklist for you as you venture into starting a company or joining a startup. Starting your own business is an exciting, enriching process; you will learn much about yourself. It will be a very rewarding journey, whatever the end result.

I plan to write several additional books to help you with other questions that will arise as your company develops—questions about raising money, hiring and recruiting talent, go-to market strategies, and managing your board and investors. This learning process works best when it is shared, so I invite you to write to me and share your stories, advice, and ideas. In this way, others may benefit from your insight and experiences. Please write to me at naeem@startup-advisor.com.

I look forward to meeting you at one of my seminars or clinics very soon.

Naeem Zafar
Silicon Valley, CA

Naeem Zafar

NAEEM ZAFAR is a member of the faculty of Haas Business School at the University of California, Berkeley, where he teaches Entrepreneurship and Innovation as part of the MBA program. He has also lectured on business, innovation, and entrepreneurship at UCLA, Brown University, Dalian Technical University in China, and several other universities in Turkey, India, Pakistan, Japan, and Singapore.

Naeem is a serial entrepreneur, having started his first business at the age of 26. He has gone on to start or work at six other startup companies. He has extensive experience as a mentor and coach to entrepreneurs and CEOs and is the founder of Concordia Ventures, a company that educates and advises entrepreneurs and startups on all aspects of starting and running a business.

Naeem most recently served as president and CEO of Pyxis Technology Inc., a company specializing in advanced chip-design software for nanometer technology. He has also been president and CEO of two other technology startups, Silicon Design Systems and Veridicom (a Bell Labs spinoff that invented the silicon fingerprint sensors found today on most laptops). Naeem has held senior marketing and engineering positions at several companies, including Quickturn Design Systems, which had an IPO in 1993 and grew to $125 million in revenues.

Naeem obtained a bachelor of science degree (*magna cum laude*) in electrical engineering from Brown University in Rhode Island, and he also has a master's degree in electrical engineering from the University of Minnesota.

Naeem is a charter member of TiE (www.TiE.org) and a charter member of OPEN (www.OPENSiliconValley.org), where he currently serves as president. He also serves on the advisory boards of several startup companies. As a part of his global entrepreneurial practice, Naeem is involved with microfinance ventures and social entrepreneurship.

Naeem's experience in starting his own businesses as well as advising hundreds of entrepreneurs and dozens of startups puts him in a unique position to help others succeed.

To contact Naeem about this book or his mentoring service, e-mail him at naeem@startup-advisor.com.